Semiotic Psychology

Berkeley Insights in Linguistics and Semiotics

Irmengard Rauch
General Editor

Vol. 26

PETER LANG
New York • Washington, D.C./Baltimore • Boston
Bern • Frankfurt am Main • Berlin • Vienna • Paris

Norman Markel

Semiotic Psychology

Speech as an Index of Emotions and Attitudes

Foreword by Cynthia Gallois

PETER LANG
New York • Washington, D.C./Baltimore • Boston
Bern • Frankfurt am Main • Berlin • Vienna • Paris

Library of Congress Cataloging-in-Publication Data

Markel, Norman Nathan.
Semiotic psychology: speech as an index
of emotions and attitudes/ Norman Markel.
p. cm. — (Berkeley insights in linguistics and semiotics; vol. 26)
Includes bibliographical references and index.
1. Psycholinguistics. 2. Speech. 3. Semiotics—Psychological aspects.
4. Content analysis (Communication). I. Title. II. Series.
BF455.M3355 401'.9—dc20 95-26227
ISBN 0-8204-3099-4
ISSN 0893-6935

Die Deutsche Bibliothek-CIP-Einheitsaufnahme

Markel, Norman Nathan:
Semiotic psychology: speech as an index of emotions and attitudes/
Norman Markel. –New York; Washington, D.C./Baltimore; Boston; Bern;
Frankfurt am Main; Berlin; Vienna; Paris: Lang.
(Berkeley insights in linguistics and semiotics; Vol. 26)
ISBN 0-8204-3099-4
NE: GT

The paper in this book meets the guidelines for permanence and durability
of the Committee on Production Guidelines for Book Longevity
of the Council of Library Resources.

Printed in the United States of America.

For Dale

"The existence of human consciousness and purpose introduces a type of complexity into the operations of human society that is not found in the rest of nature."

Eleanor Leacock

Table of Contents

Foreword

Contemporary View of Semiotic Psychology

Preliminary Observations

This book represents a special kind of history. First, it recounts the history of an academic discipline. *Semiotic Psychology* explores a body of psychological research, from the 1930s, 1940s, and 1950s, that focuses on naturally occurring language and its meanings. It provides an understanding of the theoretical and methodological backdrop of a body of research, undertaken at a time when social and clinical psychology were still strongly linked to psychophysics, on the one hand, and to psychoanalysis, on the other. Much of this research has been forgotten today, and reading the book makes us aware of how forward-thinking and in many ways ahead of their time the scholars who produced it were.

Second, this book presents a very selective history. The classic studies reviewed do not contain any examples of experimental work. Nevertheless, much such work in the 1950s using the semantic differential is in the domain of semiotic psychology. Two examples of this category of research are the experimental examination of the impact of language spoken on the meanings of words for bilinguals (Lambert, Havelka, & Crosby, 1959) and the seminal study by Lambert and his colleagues which employed the matched guise technique to examine the role of language attitudes in judgments of personality (Lambert, Gardner, Hodgson, & Fillenbaum, 1960). In contrast, *Semiotic Psychology* provides accounts of interactional talk, in interviews, conversations, or written works. The emphasis on analysis of texts was an important step in this research, and has begun to reemerge in social psychology only in recent times (see Potter & Wetherell, 1987; Coupland, Coupland, & Giles, 1991).

Third, although semiotic psychology is probably most relevant to social psychologists, much of the research described in this book comes from clinical psychology, and was partly aimed at providing tools for the diagnosis of various pathological conditions. Three of the six classic studies use clinical samples. The book shows the tradition in clinical psychology to gain insights from psychopathology, and in particular from Freudian theory, about normal psychological functioning, and to explore the important role of communication in both. Mainstream social psychology abandoned this approach for many years, largely because there was inadequate control of the differences between clinical and general population groups, although the use of clinical samples has remained a central part of the method of personality and family psychology. These early studies show, however, how the same methods can examine texts as diverse as plays and initial psychiatric interviews, and that the resulting language samples also contain striking similarities. Through their basis in psychoanalysis, they also illuminate the impact of cultural forces on thinking, emotion, attitude, and communication.

Overall, this book shows the foundations of semiotic psychology, including its methodological and theoretical origins in psychology and anthropological linguistics. It draws together the major threads underlying the classic studies, presenting theories that may never have appeared together before. Markel describes the work as if it were contemporary, leaving readers to draw their own lessons and conclusions. The remainder of this foreword chapter contains some of mine.

What Is Semiotic Psychology?

Markel defines semiotic psychology as "the scientific study of speech as an index of emotions and attitudes." In this definition, he paraphrases and combines definitions by Sebeok (1977) in comparative psychology and Jakobson (1960) in linguistics. At the same time, his conception of semiotic psychology departs somewhat from Saussure's (1974) idea of semiotics as "the life of signs in society."

Saussure's concern, and that of the semioticians who followed him, was with the structural analysis of signs. Structuralist focus is primarily on the rules of substitution (paradigmatic relations), rules of combination (syntagmatic relations), and the ways in which signs create meaning (Culler, 1976; Saussure, 1974; Morris, 1971). Saussure viewed the sign as the product of culture, the result of a learning process that united a signifier and a signified. However, in spite of his understanding a sign to be a social construction, Saussure insisted on studying sign systems isolated from the social conditions and relationships that created them. For this reason, Saussure's version of structuralism is the target of criticism both for its emphasis on *langue* (idealized language) rather than *parole* (language as it is spoken), and for its extraction of sign systems from their social and historical context. Indeed, post-structuralist analysis in cultural studies represents a strong reaction against this approach (see Culler, 1976; Hodge & Kress, 1988; and, Potter & Wetherell, 1987, for discussions of this issue). Other scholars, including Hymes (1972) in anthropology and Halliday (1978) and Hodge and Kress (1988) in linguistics, have walked a middle way, incorporating many features of structuralism into theories that nevertheless give a central role to context and to socio-structural forces.

The methods and theories presented in this book anticipate but do not articulate the later addition of social context and social forces to the analysis of signs. The research reviewed focuses on *performance* and demonstrates a major effort by the scholars of that era to bring elegance and simplicity to the enormously complex task of analyzing face-to-face interaction. Perhaps what is more important, this research insists on a paradigm that includes among its variables speech, emotions, and attitudes. In other words, an essential feature of semiotic psychology is that it looks at speech *behavior* in the context of social and clinical *psychology*. At the same time, the following pages indicate a field of study that is firmly committed to semiotics in that linguistic and paralinguistic signs are always viewed as *indices* of mental states. In this context, the chapters on language and paralanguage perform a dual function. On the one hand, these chapters provide an introduction to descriptive linguistics, and at the same time they provide a model of the structuralist enterprise.

In spite of its reliance on semiotic methods, the social science foundation of semiotic psychology is unashamedly psychological. As noted above, it draws heavily on clinical psychology, but ends up situated firmly in social psychology, striving to explain the conversational behavior of ordinary people in everyday contexts. The focus is on individuals and the ways in which these individuals negotiate the social environment. There is also a strong emphasis on internal psychological states (thinking, emotion, attitude), as these are constructed and represented in speech. This central concern with social or clinical psychological variables differentiates semiotic psychology from the closely related fields of social semiotics (Hodge & Kress, 1988) and discourse analysis (Potter & Wetherell, 1987). Since semiotic psychology conceptualizes social and cultural forces as working through the language and speech of individuals in interaction with each other, interactions cannot be thought of as texts in isolation from their originators. As such, this field of study has some themes in common with later theories in social psychology, including social identity theory (Tajfel & Turner, 1979) and communication accommodation theory (Giles & Coupland, 1991). These themes will not appeal to everyone. Even so, it would be hard for any social psychologist not to applaud the appreciation in this early work that individuals cannot be studied apart from their social environments, their speech communities, and their culture. This insight was almost lost to psychology for quite a long time.

Why a Book on Semiotic Psychology?

Readers may ask themselves an obvious question: what is the current relevance of *Semiotic Psychology* when so much has happened in psychology since the research reviewed here was published? Early trends and insights aside, what does this theory and research have to say to contemporary social psychologists that they do not already know? We find the answers to these questions in the history of social psychology and more particularly the psychology of language, *after* the period covered in this book; that is, in the 1960s and 1970s.

Early Interest in the Psychology of Language

In the late 1950s, the label "psycholinguistics" was applied to an emerging academic discipline that encompassed phonology, syntax, and semantics on the language side, and cognition, affect, and communicative behavior on the psychological side (see Ball, Gallois, & Callan, 1989). *Psycholinguistics* by Osgood and Sebeok (1954) and Roger Brown's *Words and Things* (1958) are landmark publications that put forward an integrated approach to the psychology of language. Also central to this field were the works of Hall (1959), who began a semiotic analysis of nonverbal behavior, as well as the seminal work of Brown and Gilman (1960) on power and solidarity, which has flourished only in recent times. An indication that psycholinguistics had at this moment emerged as a distinct discipline was Markel's 1961 academic appointment that bore the title "assistant professor of psycholinguistics."

The Chomskyan revolution of the 1960s eliminated the semiotic trend from psycholinguistics. Experimental psychologists whose focus was language behavior were enchanted by the elegance of Chomsky's (1957, 1965) analysis of language and his proposal of an innate human language acquisition device. Chomsky's theory provided a plethora of hypotheses about the encoding and decoding of syntax, and the approach was very well suited to the developing interest in information processing among experimental psychologists. Chomsky's focus on syntax to the exclusion of semantics, along with the emphasis in his work on idealized competence (*langue*) rather than actual performance (*parole*), was carried over into psycholinguistics. Cognitive psycholinguists began to test hypotheses about the processing of sentences, and developmental psycholinguists concentrated on the acquisition of first language syntax. As a consequence, psycholinguistics rapidly became isolated from social and clinical psychology. Not long afterward, the anthropologists, linguists, and psychologists who shared mutual interests in what Sapir had described as "speech as a personality trait" lost psycholinguistics as their interdisciplinary forum.

At the same time, the rise of social cognition saw a turning away from language and communication by most mainstream social psychologists throughout the 1960s and 1970s (McGuire, 1973). Interest centered on the way people think about social events and make social judgments and decisions; attribution theory (Jones, Kanouse, Kelley, Nisbett, Valins, & Weiner, 1972; Kelley, 1972) led this trend. The accent was on social processes, particularly intra-individual processes, and away from social meaning. Social psychology textbooks no longer contained chapters on language, communication, or even the influence of culture. This study was left to other fields.

The study of the social influences on language was mainly taken over by sociology and linguistics, with the result that psychological factors and the role of mental states were played down, while the influence of macro-level factors (social class, gender, race, and at the lower limit social networks) was played up. Linguistics, particularly sociolinguistics, never abandoned the study of actual spoken language and its variability, as the work of Labov (1966) and others attests. Even in the study of syntax, the role of the social environment was not completely neglected (Fillmore, 1968), as grammar based on theories of action, or what later came to be called cognitive grammar, began to develop in opposition to Chomskyan transformational grammar (Langacker, 1990). On the other hand, sociolinguists were not very interested in psychological variables such as attitude and affect.

Overall, the study of the social psychology of language and communication virtually disappeared from psychology. Researchers in the field of communication studies during this period began to adopt the empirical methodology of the behavioral sciences, and to incorporate theory from social psychology into their own work. Understandably enough, they concentrated on current theorizing, and as a result lost much of the earlier emphasis on semiotics. The few researchers in social psychology who continued to work in the area were mainly Lambert and his colleagues in Canada (Lambert, 1967; Gardner & Lambert, 1972); and Giles and his colleagues in the United

Kingdom (e.g., Giles, 1973; Giles & Powesland, 1975). Lambert and Giles retained the earlier interest in attitudes, but lost the emphasis on spontaneous speech, and adopted an experimental methodology where language variables were controlled and manipulated.

Research in nonverbal communication, conducted by a small number of social and clinical psychologists along with researchers in communication studies and speech science, probably retained the strongest links with the past. Birdwhistell's (1952f, 1970) early attempt to use the methods of structural linguistics as a method of systematizing research into gesture (or the science of kinesics) was echoed in detailed studies of courtship behavior in psychotherapy (Scheflen, 1965), greeting behavior (Kendon, 1970), and so forth. Markel's own work on the expression of personality in voice qualities (Markel, Meisels, & Houck, 1964; Markel, 1965; Markel, Phillis, Vargas, & Howard, 1972), and speaking time (Gallois & Markel, 1975; Markel, Bein, & Phillis, 1973), showed a strong semiotic influence, and anticipated some of the work of Scherer (1978, 1979, 1988). Even here, however, most of the field moved away from semiotics, and from the analysis of spontaneous behavior, in favor of experimental research exploring the process and function of nonverbal communication, rather than its meaning (Argyle & Dean, 1965; Exline, 1971). Argyle (1988) reviews this research functional and meaning centered approaches to the study of nonverbal communication.

Present Day Trends

By the mid- to late 1970s, the work described in *Semiotic Psychology* had been forgotten by all but a few researchers, and its influence had been eclipsed by that of Chomsky, on the one hand, and social cognition, on the other. In addition, the study of language and communication was fragmented and spread thinly across several of the social sciences and humanities (at least sociology, anthropology, education, communication studies, linguistics, media studies, cultural studies, and psychology), as well as across several subfields of psychology. Then, the pendulum began to swing back, with a sudden increase in interest in the social psychology of language (Giles & St. Clair,

1979; Scherer & Giles, 1979), speech act theory (Grice, 1975; Searle, 1969, 1979), and nonverbal communication (Rosenthal, 1979; Rosenthal, et al., 1979), which has continued to the present day.

Unfortunately, a number of key features of the earlier work had been lost. First, researchers had lost the common language and concepts of the past, which hindered them in developing methods for observing, recording, and analyzing spoken language. In recent times much interest has centered on text and discourse analysis. In this context, content analysis has been strongly criticized for the grossness of its categories and its lack of attention to the relational aspects of language (Potter & Wetherell, 1987). The systems of content analysis described in *Semiotic Psychology* were much subtler, richer, and more systematic than most of the versions current today, and they provide many clues for present-day researchers who wish to study meaning.

In addition, present-day quantitative methods for studying spontaneous language and nonverbal behavior are poor at the level of data coding. This deficit is partly because psychologists of the current generation lack the knowledge of syntax and semantics that would provide a detailed analysis of these language variables. Several of the classic studies described in this book show the ways in which speech communication can be quantified using linguistic and paralinguistic methods. This process gives important insights to contemporary researchers, even though the statistical techniques of the earlier period are out-dated and have been replaced. Some of the hostility towards traditional psychological methods shown by discourse analysts in sociology, linguistics, and even social psychology undoubtedly stems from the lack of sophistication in behavioral coding. Perhaps what is more important, the classic studies in this book show how psychological and linguistic analyses can be combined to produce coding systems that take account of both aspects of behavior; that is, a semiotically based analysis.

Contribution of This Book

In the Introduction to the book, five literature reviews are presented as defining the field of semiotic psychology. The choice of these particular five articles is noteworthy in that there is little overlap among the research studies presented in them. Few researchers today would group these five reviews together as representing different dimensions of one field of study. Indeed, few are likely to be well acquainted with all of them, which reflects the fragmentation of the field. In choosing them, Markel makes clear his focus on the relation between speech and personality, his use of the methods of structural linguistics, his emphasis on the role of culture, and his interest in nonverbal as well as verbal behavior. The domain of the field he describes is large.

Learning Theory

The early chapters of *Semiotic Psychology* are devoted to a detailed and very accessible description of the theories that influenced the classic studies reported later. Learning theory, and in particular Pavlovian conditioning, is linked to sign theory and general semantics. Sign theory and general semantics are models that are essential for understanding the theoretical foundations of the studies reviewed. Of course, learning theory, both classical and operant conditioning, has a central place in psychology, but the application of principles of learning to language and communication has had its ups and downs. Skinner proposed a radical version of it in *Verbal Behavior* (1956). For many, Chomskyan theory buried this analysis of language and its acquisition in about 1960. It never really died, however. Researchers in nonverbal communication like Argyle (1988) and Siegman and Feldstein (1987) continued to make implicit use of conditioning principles in their work. In addition, Skinnerian behaviorism, with its catch-cry "behavior is determined by its consequences," flourished in clinical psychology, including training in social and communication skills.

Only very recently have behaviorist accounts of social behavior returned to the fore. In one such account, Guerin (1994) explores the crucial impact of the social context on language and communication, among other social behaviors. The kind of associationism Markel describes has changed dramatically over the years, but his account is still important for understanding the studies he reviews. In addition, the link made between learning theory and semiotics, which automatically makes central both socially determined signs and the impact of the social context, as well as his provocative account of consciousness and consciousness-raising, should prove extremely useful for anyone who wants to think about language as learned behavior.

Personal and Social Identity

Markel takes the principles of learning theory into an explanation of the formation of stereotypes and thence to a consideration of prejudice. It is interesting that he does this, as none of the studies reviewed later is overtly concerned with prejudice. In doing this, however, he shows the connection between self-concept and personality, stereotypes, attitudes, and prejudice, particularly as they are signalled in language and nonverbal communication. He also brings out the strong connections between personality and culture, as well as among motivation, emotion, and power and solidarity. These connections have been all too often ignored in modern research, although there are recent indications that they are being recognized again (for example, Gallois, 1994; Ng & Bradac, 1993; Triandis, 1994).

The lesson here is that the methods used in the classic studies, which in the main were explorations of personality and affective states, are equally applicable in studies of social identity (Tajfel & Turner, 1979; Turner, 1987) and language attitudes. One measure Markel describes in detail, the semantic differential, has of course been used widely in studies of prejudice and language attitudes. Reviews of these semantic differential studies are to be found in Giles and Coupland (1991) and Ryan and Giles (1982). Harper, Wiens, and Matarazzo (1978) review observational and content analysis techniques and indicate that these techniques have been used mainly in studies of personality, interpersonal communication, and in clinical settings. It should be noted that these techniques could be used equally well in studies of intergroup communication. In fact, research in interpersonal communication and research in intergroup communication have continued as two independent traditions, with little crossover between them. The recent work of Giles and his colleagues (Coupland, Coupland, Giles, &

Henwood, 1988; Coupland, Coupland, & Giles,1991; Gallois, Franklyn-Stokes, Giles, & Coupland, 1988) has begun to reverse this trend; however, they have relied mainly on discourse analysis to examine the interpersonal aspects of communication in intergroup settings. The present book points to a different but compatible approach: a more clearly semiotic analysis.

Language and Paralanguage

In preparing the ground for the classic studies, Markel also discusses the important relationships between verbal and nonverbal behavior, and in particular between language and paralanguage. He draws on the work of Sapir (1927) and Trager (1958) to show how language and paralanguage can be studied using the same methods; psychologists should pay attention to these methodological points, which we have never really understood. Markel also brings to our attention Sapir's ideas about the inter-connection between verbal and nonverbal communication, exemplified in Sapir's notion that the physical characteristics of the articulation of some words are related to their meaning. For example, Sapir notes that the vowel sound "a," which uses a relatively large opening in the mouth for its articulation, appears often in words denoting "largeness," while the sound "i," which is small, often denotes smallness; Markel's study of the psychomorph explored this idea empirically (Markel & Hamp, 1965). Although empirical research has shown that this relationship between sound and meaning is fairly rough, the underlying idea that there is no absolute separation between language signs, the accompanying nonverbal behavior, the meaning, and the society that generated them all, is again returning to prominence (see Hodge & Kress, 1988).

The Classic Studies

The six classic studies are reviewed in wonderful detail. They are astonishing in the simplicity of their conceptualization, and for the way they apply ideas from learning theory, Freudian theory, and structural linguistics straight to the analysis of data. At the same time, each one of them is completely systematic, avoiding the temptation to leave data coding half-done, or to take the easy way out in coding. In this, they anticipate the return in recent years to careful analysis of discourse (Potter & Wetherell, 1987). Present-day researchers in psychology will gain a deeper understanding of the psychological approach to this type of analysis by examining its history.

Each of the studies contributes something different. One shows the use of dramatic texts to provide information about ordinary conversation. Another compares the use of more direct and indirect syntax (see Semin & Fiedler, 1988, for a recent application of this idea to the area of prejudice). The studies give detailed comparisons of people with different psychopathological conditions or, alternatively, different personality types, showing more detailed analyses of the language of these people than we are likely to come across today. Finally, the studies demonstrate the use of idiographic or nomothetic methods, although it must be said that the nomothetic example, while it employs statistical inference, only includes four subjects and may not be considered nomothetic by some researchers.

All six studies provide a rich source of research ideas, many of which have never been followed up, as well as a mine of research methods for modern researchers. They also point to the problems inherent in doing this kind of research, although Markel does not deal with this issue in any detail. It is no accident that so few studies of this type have been published; they are extremely hard and time-consuming to conduct (Potter & Wetherell, 1987, make this point about discourse analysis). For example, the study by Soskin and John required over a year of full-time work on transcription and coding alone, and this for only four people. The transcription for *The First Five Minutes* similarly took hundreds of hours—for the first five minutes of an interview between two people.

Given the constraints on academics to publish, it is not surprising that researchers have been tempted to abandon these rigorous methods and even to argue that simpler methods, like questionnaires or simple rating systems, can give us most of the same information. Clearly, as these studies show, this is not the case. Researchers must make a choice, either to look seriously at the way language works in discourse or not to. If they choose to do so, this book will help them a great deal, by showing how earlier scholars made the immense task manageable. Markel's choice to put the earlier studies last, indeed, highlights how simpler methods can produce very rich results.

Conclusion

As noted above, this book is a special kind of history. It puts us in touch with a forgotten tradition in content analysis and the observation of spontaneous communication. It also shows the close links between psychology and linguistics that are so important to systematic study of discourse, and which are being re-discovered in recent times. For me, the book provides a concise summary of a body of research that is larger than I had thought. It also draws out the similarities in what are superficially very diverse studies, not the least because they were published in totally different places. The book gives us many imaginative ideas for strengthening our own research, especially in the observation of behavior and data coding.

Even more importantly, this book links a varied body of literature into a new field, by showing how all of it is semiotic in focus. It does not give us a research agenda, but it points toward one, in which social and personal meanings are explored *together* in language and communication. Psychologists have been striking in their resistance to undertaking this task, preferring to concentrate either on personal and interpersonal factors or on intergroup ones (Giles & Coupland, 1991, are a partial exception). The work reviewed here shows the potential of examining, for example, racism or sexism, simultaneously on the personal and social level. Semiotic psychology opens up the possibility of theorizing this study, something that is sorely lacking today. These studies leave us with a set of concepts and methods that will be useful for many years to come.

Cynthia Gallois
Department of Psychology
The University of Queensland, Australia

ods. Marsella et al. have put the reader and researcher ahead [illegible] [illegible] unmatched [illegible].

Conclusion

[illegible] the [illegible] this book is [illegible] with a forgotten [illegible] of [illegible] of [illegible] and [illegible] important [illegible] study of [illegible]. For [illegible] thought [illegible] what are [illegible] not the least because they were published [illegible] places. The book [illegible] us many [illegible] observations [illegible] coding.

[illegible] importantly, this book takes [illegible] into a new field by [illegible]. It [illegible] research [illegible] to [illegible] and [illegible] meaning [illegible] in [illegible] and [illegible] of [illegible] personal and [illegible] group [illegible] of [illegible]. The [illegible] book shows the [illegible] of [illegible] for [illegible] the personal and social [illegible] psychology [illegible] of [illegible] this study [illegible] These studies [illegible] will be useful for many years to come.

Cynthia Gallois
Department of Psychology
The University of Queensland, Australia

Introduction

A. The Title

In a passage devoted to developmental zoosemiotics, Sebeok provides a functional example that defines the study of semiotic psychology (Sebeok, 1977):

> It has been shown that . . . one dominant sign of senescence in our culture, 'repetitiousness,' . . . contrary to the usual assumption that this tedious habit is simply a symptom of physiological deterioration in old folks, . . . is rather a semiotic manifestation of an adaptive strategy useful to the elderly in capturing an audience. (p. 317)

In other words, a particular speech sign behavior (repetitiousness) is the manifestation of a mental state (adaptive strategy). In this pithy example Sebeok captures the essence of semiotic psychology: the study of speech sign behavior as an index of a mental state.

Roman Jakobson, in a chapter devoted to the analysis of poetry, also writes of speech signs as manifestations of mental states and elucidates the nature of the mental states involved (Jakobson, 1960). Under the rubric "emotive," Jakobson combines the mental states emotion and attitude, which are, psychologically speaking, the pleasant-unpleasant and the pro-con dimensions of affect, respectively.

> The so-called *emotive* or 'expressive' function [of language], focused on the *addresser*, aims a direct expression of the speaker's attitude toward what he [/she] is speaking about. It tends to produce an impression of a certain emotion whether true or feigned: therefore the term 'emotive,' . . . has proved to be preferable to 'emotional'. (p. 354, emphases in the original)

Jakobson's definition of "the emotive function of language," indicates the same focus as the Sebeok example: the study of speech sign behavior ("speaking") as an expression of a mental state ("speaker's attitude" and "certain emotion"). Jakobson's term "emotive," by combining emotion and attitude, indicates that he viewed semiotic psychology as being related to two domains of psychological interest: personality (emotions) and social psychology (attitudes).

Consolidation of these assertions by Sebeok and Jakobson yields the following definition:[1] Semiotic psychology is the discipline devoted to the scientific study of speech as an index of emotions and attitudes.

In the present context the vital semiotic concept *index* "refers to membership-identifying characteristics of a group, such as regional, social, or occupational markers; . . . [or] to such physiological, psychological, or social features of speech or writing that reveal personal characteristics" (Sebeok, 1990, p. 22).

B. The Purpose

There have been, over the years, including an innovative programmatic statement by Sapir, five literature reviews summarizing research that focuses on speech signs as expressions of emotions and attitudes. These publications, which functionally define the domain of "semiotic psychology," identify their subject matter as:

- "Speech as a Personality Trait" (Sapir, 1927)
- "Speech and Personality" (Sanford, 1942)
- "Linguistic Aspects of Cross-Cultural Personality Study" (Hymes, 1961)
- "Psychological Research in the Extralinguistic Area" (Mahl & Schulze, 1964)
- "The Telltale Voice: Nonverbal Messages of Verbal Communication" (Siegman, 1978/1987)

The large amount of research proposed and summarized in these articles points to an "ology," that is, a body of knowledge with similar theoretical biases and research paradigms. This "ology" is being pursued by scholars from the diverse fields of anthropology, clinical psychology, linguistics, psychiatry, and social psychology. The disparate titles of these five articles indicate that this "ology" has not coalesced under one banner.

However, the focus of each of these articles is quite clearly speech as an index of emotions and attitudes.

There is today no single source that provides a comprehensive foundation for the study of speech as an index of emotions and attitudes. This book attempts to fill this need by providing in one volume the fundamental assumptions and the research methods that make an "ology" of semiotic psychology.

C. The Content

1. The Psychology of Sign Behavior

Part I, The Psychology of Sign Behavior, provides the social science context of semiotic psychology. The interdisciplinary nature of the study of semiotic psychology will be evident from the integration of relevant knowledge from experimental psychology, social psychology, and personality theory. Part I begins with a discussion of Pavlov and his famous learning experiment on dogs (Chapter 1: Thinking), proceeds through the study of attitudes, which is the core of social psychology (Chapter 2: Emotive States: I), and ends with a description of power and solidarity (Chapter 3: Emotive States II).

Thinking and Emotive States are psychological topics that the science of semiotic psychology shares with any discipline that is concerned with speech signs. However, it is the inclusion of emotions and attitudes that differentiates semiotic psychology from other closely related disciplines (for example, sociolinguistics, psycholinguistics, neurolinguistics, and anthropological linguistics).

There are three reasons for the range across usually segregated fields of psychology: First, sign behavior does not drop from the sky; it is learned behavior. A model of the basic operations for learning speech signs is fundamentally the same as a model that aids in understanding how Dr. Pavlov's dogs learned to raise their paws to the sound of a buzzer. Second, the central hypothesis of the science of semiotic psychology is that speech signs are the objective behavioral indices of subjective mental states. And third, the primary concern of research in semiotic psychology is the study of speech signs in the context of social communication. In this context emotions and attitudes regarding power and solidarity are important psychological factors conditioning the expression and interpretation of speech signs.

2. Speech Signs

In Part II: Speech Signs, we leave the domain of mental states as viewed by experimental psychology, social psychology, and personality theory, and enter the domain of vocal performance as categorized by structural linguists. The two chapters in this part provide an understanding of the specific units of analysis that will be encountered in research that focuses on speech sign behavior. One or more of the linguistic or paralinguistic units described in this part will be found in any semiotic psychology study, regardless of the academic discipline of the author. There is no mention in this part of Noam Chomsky or the research he has inspired because transformational linguistics, which focuses on linguistic competence, is not encountered in the semiotic psychology literature.

Speech consists of signs that are either language or paralanguage. Chapter 4, "Linguistic signs" describes phonetics, phonemics, morphemics, syntax, and semantics. These are structural levels of analysis, that describe how the words of a language are produced and put together to make meaningful sentences. Then Chapter 5, "Paralinguistic Signs," provides a method for describing those non-language sounds which may occur either simultaneously with or between words.

3. Semiotic Psychology

Part III, Semiotic Psychology describes the research paradigms and the classic experiments in the scientific study of speech signs as expressions of emotions and attitudes.

The study of speech sign behavior employs both idiographic and nomothetic research paradigms. The idiographic point of view studies the speech signs of a single speaker in relation to other speech signs produced by that speaker. The nomothetic point of view examines speech signs in terms of their differential use by different speakers.

The idiographic method is the approach of the anthropological linguist who is primarily concerned with the speech signs of one individual and how these speech signs compare with each other. In examining the voice quality of loudness, the concern of the anthropological linguist is first establishing a norm or "base line" for the individual speaker and then noting those places where individuals depart from their base line. "The First Five Minutes" described in detail in Chapter 6, is an example of an idiographic research project.

The nomothetic method is the approach of the social psychologist, whose primary concern is how one individual compares with another individual in the use of a particular speech sign. Thus, in examining the voice quality of loudness, the concern of the social psychologist is establishing a continuum of loudness on which all speakers are compared and then noting the placement of different speakers on this continuum. "The Study of Spontaneous Talk," described in detail in Chapter 7, is an example of a nomothetic research project.

The guide for identifying the classic experiments presented in Chapter 8 was reference to three early comprehensive reviews of the literature. The first was published in 1942 by Sanford, a social psychologist. The second was published in 1961 by Hymes, an anthropological linguist, in a book entitled *Studying Personality Cross-Culturally*. The third was published in 1964 by Mahl, a clinical psychologist, and his student, Schulze, and appeared in a book entitled *Approaches to Semiotics*. The Newman and Mather, Balken and Masserman, and Boder articles are the only research referenced in all three of these reviews. Sanford's review does not refer to his own research article; however, it is referred to by both Hymes and Mahl and Schulze.

After general comments, Chapter 8 opens with a synthesis and abridgment of two articles by Newman and Mather (Newman & Mather, 1938; Newman, 1939). The first article (Newman & Mather, 1938) details the methodology used in both the 1938 and 1939 articles. Newman was Sapir's student, and the methodology described in the earlier publication is the first published application of the methodology described by Sapir in his 1927 article, "Speech as a Personality Trait."

The indication of the link between psychiatry and the study of speech signs is the extensive documentation of the clinical case histories included in the first article. However, there is nothing that can be described as a "review of the literature" in either the Newman and Mather or the Newman article. Between these two articles the only reference to any previous work is the reference to Malinowski's concept of "phatic communication." Be that as it may, it is possible to glimpse Newman's philosophic stance and his goals in the first part of the second article that is abridged below. Here we read that his interest in this research was to operationalize, in the form of objective measures, the indexical function of language and paralanguage.

The abridgment of Balken and Masserman's work, which is also a synthesis of two articles, is presented next in Chapter 8 (Masserman & Balkan, 1939; Masserman, 1940). The fact that Masserman is a psychiatrist and Balkan a clinical psychologist indicates the interdisciplinary aspect of their collaboration. Apparently Balken and Masserman were aware of the importance of paralinguistic variables in the expression of emotion. In citing the work of Davis (1935) as being closely related to their own work, they state that Davis had postulated "that inherent in the sound of different letters of the alphabet there are qualities of personality of character." This was an early version of the 'constant content' method of research, which is specifically designed to evaluate the role of voice qualities and vocal qualifiers by controlling content. However, in practice, none of the measures they applied to their speech samples included any aspect of paralanguage. The absence of a linguistic anthropologist on this project may account for the lack of any phonetic or phonemic variables in their measurement procedures. In this vein, it is consistent that Balken and Masserman do not refer to Sapir's 1927 article "Speech as a Personality Trait."

The absence of an anthropologist and the presence of a psychologist, perhaps adds another important difference between the work of Balken and Masserman, on the one hand, and that of Newman and Mather, on the other. The latter, especially Newman's solo article, indicates an interest in speech signs in a broad social communication context, whereas the former appear to be primarily interested in the diagnostic value of the various lexical indices they developed. In spite of their caveats as to the diagnostic uses of the results of their research in psychiatric practice, psychological diagnosis is an obvious practical application of the work of Balken and Masserman.

Boder's research (1940), which is the third study to be reviewed in abridged form in Chapter 8, disseminated the work of Busemann (1925) to the scholarly community in the United States. Boder's work, originally master's thesis research, was published ten years after being submitted for his degree, and he cites demand for the original research as the impetus for his finally making the material available in published form. There is evidence for this demand in that Balkan and Masserman, as well as Sanford, cite Boder's work, the former authors referring specifically to the M.A. thesis.

Newman and Mather do not refer to either Busemann's Action Quotient or Boder's Adjective-Verb Quotient. Balkan and Masserman, however, employ the Adjective-Verb Quotient, and the use of quotients looms large in their methodology. This may be additional evidence for the development in anthropology (from Newman and Mather) and psychology (from Balkan and Masserman) of separate and independent research strategies, the former at Yale and the latter at Chicago. In a historical context, it is noteworthy that Sapir taught at both institutions during the period that both types of research were in progress.

Chapter 8 concludes with the work of Sanford, who published two important articles in 1942. One was a literature review article entitled "Speech and Personality" (1942a). The other bears the title "Speech and Personality: A Comparative Case Study" (1942b). Sanford was the first practitioner of semiotic psychology to bring together, in an organized manner theories, methods, and results in the systematic study of the emotional and attitudinal functions of speech signs, and to define the focus of this field of study as ". . . the existence, consistency, and significance of individual differences in the mode of verbal expression" (p. 811).

The one hundred and six books and articles cited in Sanford's review of the literature are divided into nine categories: 1. studies of literary style; 2. types of speech and types of thought; 3. the language of the child; 4. semantics and the individual; 5. diagnostic significance of specific linguistic constructions; 6. effective speech and effective personality; 7. speech and psychopathology; 8. voice and personality; and 9. disorders of speech. The thread linking what seems to be, from a current perspective, nine separate and perhaps disparate fields of study, was that they all had a similar goal: the study of language and paralanguage as expressions of emotions and attitudes.

In his research article, Sanford does not give any reasons for choosing the particular linguistic or paralinguistic variables he examined. However, he appears to have wanted to examine every linguistic and paralinguistic variable that was either explicitly defined or implicitly discussed in the series of books and articles that he assimilated into his thinking for a review of the literature. This led to the project described in Chapter 8, of examining a total of 7,488 linguistic and paralinguistic variables. Given that in his time data reduction consisted of a punch-card system, one can appreciate the gargantuan task he set for himself.

"Speech and Personality: A comparative case study," is an important landmark for the study of speech as an index of emotions and attitudes. Sanford's extensive review of the relevant literature summarizes what came before it and his empirical methods indicate a program of research for semiotic psychology that has yet to be fulfilled.

PART I

THE PSYCHOLOGY OF SIGN BEHAVIOR

1

Thinking

A. Learning

1. Pavlov

The results of the work of the Russian physiologist Ivan Pavlov have led to the scientific conclusion that thinking is a function of the central nervous system. This conclusion means that the development of a brain led to the development of a 'mind.' "The brain is the organ of thought. Thinking is a function performed by the brain" (Cornforth, 1963, p. 12). Pavlov discovered that the central nervous system, in addition to functioning as a coordinator of the different systems of the body, was the means by which living organisms interact with their surroundings. The greater the development of the brain, especially the cerebral cortex, the greater the possibility the animal has of learning from interactions with its environment. In interacting with the environment, the animal employs a vast repertoire of muscular and glandular behaviors. It is, however, the brain that coordinates and controls these actions, and it does its work of coordination through the reflexes: unconditioned and conditioned.

The fundamental connection of the animal to its environment is the unconditioned reflex: a natural response (Ru) to a particular stimulus (Su). An unconditioned reflex is a fixed and automatic connection between the organism and its environment, and is part of the genetic heredity of the animal. If, for example, something suddenly passes in front of the eyes, the eye lids blink. This is the result of an Su–Ru automatic connection, which serves to protect the eye. Irrespective of the varying conditions that it encounters the animal relates itself to the surrounding world through such reflexes.

There are in addition to Rus, connections between the organism and its environment, which are brought into being during the life of the organism. These are the conditioned reflexes. A conditioned reflex (Rc) is a temporary and variable connection. If conditions change, then the connections change and the Rc can disappear. A dog can have its food at a certain place, but if its trainer changes that place, the dog can very quickly relearn where to find its food. This aspect of an Rc then contrasts sharply with an Ru on which the change of conditions has no effect.

The procedure whereby both the unconditioned response and the conditioned response are formed takes place in the central nervous system. The final connection between the sensory input and the motor output takes place in the brain and the more complex the brain–that is the more convoluted the cerebral cortex–the more complex can be the conditioned responses of the animal.

2. Conditioning

It was, then, the Russian physiologist Pavlov who, while examining the physiology of the digestive glands, discovered the phenomenon of conditioning. His insight was derived from his observation that stimuli that regularly preceded the giving of food–the food pan, the smell of the food and even the sight of the experimenter–came to elicit secretions from the dog's salivary glands. In his book *Conditioned Reflexes*, published in 1927, Pavlov reported his detailed experiments on what he called "psychic" salivation. The basic elements of the conditioning function as described by Osgood (1956) are as follows: First, there are already existing stimulus-response relationships in the animal: the Su–Ru connections mentioned in the preceding section. Conditioning takes place when the stimulus that was already existing that elicited a particular response, comes to elicit a response that was not related to it. When this happens, we say that conditioning has taken place. Figures 1.1 and 1.2 portray this situation.

After many repetitions of emitting these two behaviors in sufficiently close temporal proximity, Amos lifts his right paw upon hearing "Amos shake hands." When this has been

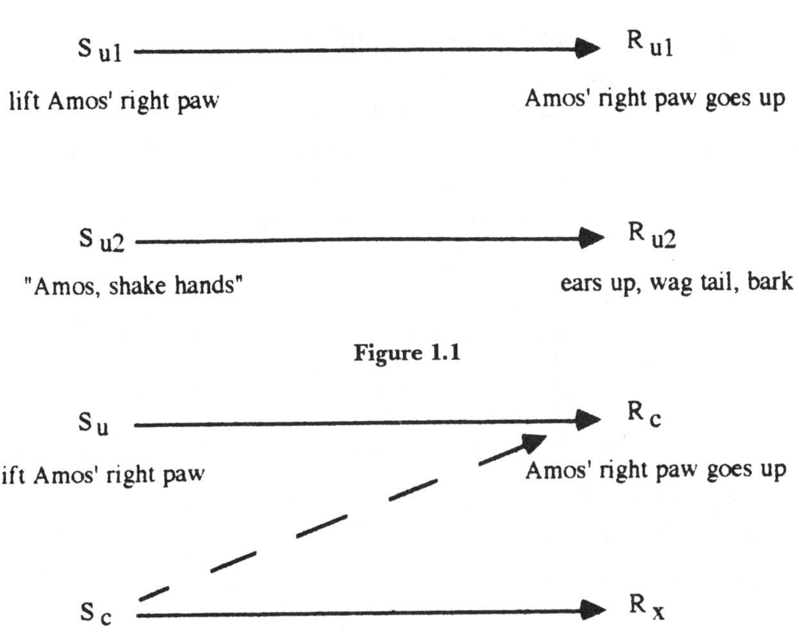

Figure 1.1

Figure 1.2

accomplished, in conditioning paradigm terminology Su1 receives the label 'conditioned stimulus' (Sc), since its ability to produce the desired reaction is conditional upon the reinforcing procedures. Su2 receives the label 'unconditioned stimulus,' and its essential characteristic is that within the given experimental situation, it regularly and without fail, produced the desired reaction. Ru2 then is the unconditioned response before the beginning of the reinforcement procedure; afterwards, when it is elicited by "Amos shake hands," it receives the label 'conditioned response' (Rc). A classic model of this whole operation is complete with the diagonal arrow indicating 'comes to elicit.'

An old proverb "the burned child avoids the flame" is a pithy summation of the principles involved in conditioning. The flicker of the flame originally elicits curiosity and approach, but after being burned, the sight of the flame elicits avoidance. The *law of conditioning* states: Whenever a stimulus has a motor outlet, any stimulus occurring simultaneously will tend to acquire the same motor outlet. After sufficient repetition (sometimes one occasion is enough) the second stimulus alone will suffice to produce a discharge in that motor outlet. The law of the conditioned reflex plus "motivation" can give a good account of personality. Allport (1961) provides an analysis of this sort.

> Suppose that a woman decorates her room in blue, is fond of blue dresses, plants many blue flowers in her garden. She has a strong general preference for blue. The developmental story in terms of conditioning might be told as [follows]. Originally: food caused an approaching (adient) response. This is an inborn, unconditioned reflex. The mother is a 'stimulus occurring simultaneously': so by the law the mother arouses approaching behavior (i.e., acquires the same 'motor outlet' as did the food). In due time other things associated with the mother (e.g., her preference for blue) become second order conditionings. The mother is perhaps now dead, but blue in any context still causes our hypothetical lady to 'approach.' Some such history of conditioning could be invoked to explain an adult's liking for pictures, vocations, churches, foods, [types] of people, philosophical or moral doctrines. (p. 93)

3. Sign Theory

In his book *Signs, Language and Behavior*, Charles Morris (1946) summarizes the philosophic parameters and the rules for discussion in the field of semiotics. His purpose was "to lay the foundation for a comprehensive and fruitful science of signs." Morris lists the names of Edward C. Tolman and Clark L. Hull, two of the giants in the early history of behaviorist psychology, as individuals whose theories had a great influence on his writing. It is logical then that Morris starts this seminal work with two stories pertaining to the law of the conditioned reflex:

> We shall begin by taking two examples of behavior to which the term 'sign' is often applied both in common usage and in the writings of semioticians. . . . If a hungry dog that goes to a certain place to obtain food when the food is seen or smelled, is trained in a certain way, it will learn to go to this place for food when a buzzer is sounded even though the food is not observed. . . . Many persons would say in such a situation that the buzzer sound is to the dog a sign of food at the given place, and in particular, a non-language sign. If we abstract from the experimenter and his purposes in this example, and consider only the dog, the example approximates what have often been called 'natural signs,' as when a dark cloud is a sign of rain. It is in this way that we wish the experiment to be considered.

> The second example is drawn from human behavior. [A person] on the way to a certain town is driving along a road; he [/she] is stopped by another person who says that the road is blocked some distance away by a landslide. The person who hears the sounds which are uttered does not continue to the point in question, but turns off on a side-road and takes another route to his[/her] destination. It would be commonly said that the sounds made by the one person and heard by the other (and indeed by the utterer also) were signs to both of them of the obstacle on the road, and in particular were language signs even though the actual responses of the two persons are very different. (p. 5)

In these two examples of the law of the conditioned reflex, both the dog and the traveler behave in a way which satisfies a need–hunger and arrival at destination, respectively. Both the buzzer and the words control behavior similar to the control that would occur if the food and the obstacle where tangibly present. That is to say, the buzzer and the words are 'substitutes' for the control over behavior in a manner similar to the control exerted by the actual food and obstacle. Because they control the course of behavior with respect to the goals of getting food and getting to a certain place in a way similar (but not necessarily exactly the same) as would the food and obstacle if they were present, the food and the buzzer are signs. The behavior which they control is called sign-behavior.

Morris points to a distinction that has important ramifications for the study of speech signs. That is that there are two types of signs: signals and symbols. A signal is a sign that has some tangible relation to that for which it substitutes. For example, a particular level of blood pressure may be interpreted by a physician as a sign of a heart condition. However this blood pressure is a signal because there is a real-world relationship between blood pressure and the functioning of the heart. However, when the physician refers to the blood pressure in words, these words are symbols.

Another demonstration of Morris' point would be to consider the signs the roman numeral III and the word 'three.' The roman numeral III is a signal because it reflects in a one-to-one way that to which it refers. If you were in a land in which you could not speak the language and wanted three apples, you could point to the basket of apples, raise three fingers, and without uttering a sound obtain three apples. The word 'three' is a symbol because it bears no relationship whatsoever to what it is referring to. In our non-English speaking merchant example, you might be standing in front of the basket of apples and say 'three,' but even increasing your loudness to a shout will not get you three apples, because the word 'three' is a symbol whose relationship to the real world is completely arbitrary. In other words, you have to learn its meaning in the same manner that Amos learned to raise his paw to "Amos shake hands."

Sign-behavior, the study of which involves every aspect of human behavior, is the focus of interest of many disciplines. Morris wrote his earlier work, *Foundations of the Theory of Signs*, as part of a large project in the philosophy of science, to provide a common terminology for all the disciplines concerned with sign-behavior. The philosophy of science purpose of his work is evident in his attempt to provide operational definitions for the crucial aspects of language behavior: terms like signal and symbol which point to very significant aspects of human language usage. Students of semiotic psychology can benefit greatly by reference to Morris' work to help them understand and to label the phenomena they are studying.

Another example of Morris' philosophy of science efforts is his identification of three types of studies of sign-behavior: pragmatics, semantics, and syntactics. 'Pragmatics' studies the relationship between signs and the users of these signs; the ways in which signs relate to the culture and personality of the speakers and listeners. 'Semantics' studies the relationship between signs and their reference. That is to say that the concern of semantics is the 'meaning' of signs. 'Syntactics' studies the relationship of signs to each other. That is, the combination of signs without regard to their meaning or as a reflection of the culture or personality of the users of the signs.

B. Meaning

1. Mediation Theory

Morris (1946) provided the following definition of a sign: "If anything, A, is a preparatory-stimulus which in the absence of stimulus-objects initiating response-sequences of a certain behavior-family causes a *disposition* in some organism to respond under certain conditions by response-sequences of this behavior-family, then A is a sign" (p. 10, emphasis added). This is technical language for 'the buzzer and the words are substitutes for the control over behavior in a manner similar to the control exerted by the actual food and obstacle.' However, a new and important word, *disposition* appears in Morris' formal definition. It has only been implied to this point, but disposition states explicitly that Morris is concerned with an underlying mental function, something going on inside the head of the animal that intervenes between the environmental stimulus (S) and the behavioral response (R). This disposition to respond is the meaning of the stimulus for the animal.

It is important to be aware of the fact that 'meaning' is an imagined mental function, which is the result of speculation. Such inferred events are referred to by psychologists as hypothetical constructs. "They are hypothetical because they are not directly observable and have been 'deduced' or 'induced' through some kind of rational or reasoning activity. They are 'constructs' because they have been 'built up' from pieces of presumed evidence and they have taken on the appearance of real *things* or 'entities'" (Bugelski, 1960, p. 47).

A portrayal of the pattern of hypothetical mental events appears in Figure 1.3. where rm–sm represents 'meaning.' Because rm-sm represents a pattern of activity

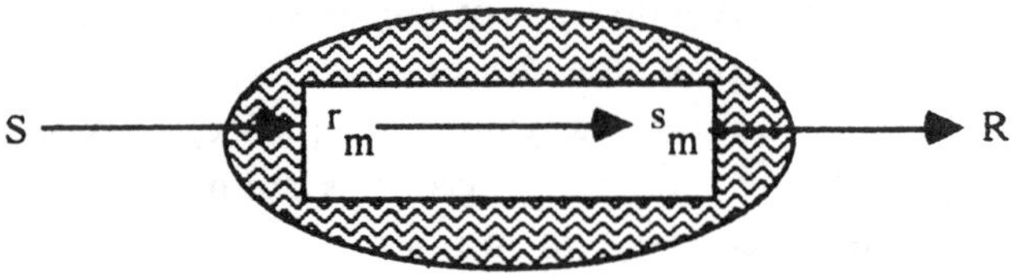

Figure 1.3

between the environmental stimulus and the behavioral response, it is labeled 'mediator,' and the process is called 'mediation.' Calling again on our trusty friend Amos, Figure 1.4 illustrates this paradigm.

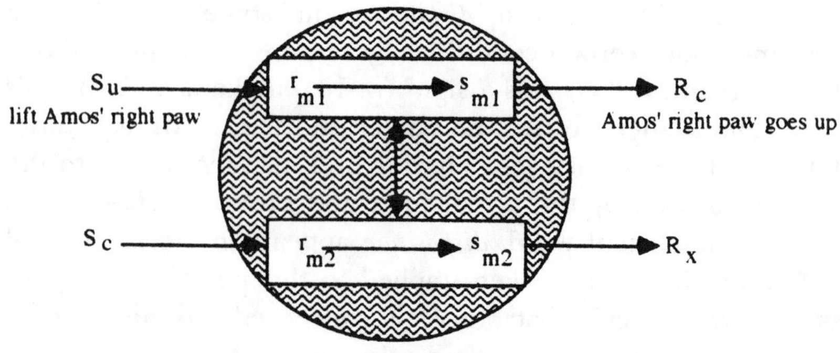

Figure 1.4

This diagram shows that the mediating process that intervenes between Su and Rc has become associated with the mediating process that intervenes between Sc and Rx. After repeated reinforcement the association becomes so strong that every time Amos hears "Amos, shake hands," Amos raises his right paw. At this point we can say that Amos knows the meaning of "Amos, shake hands." Since the Su and the Rc are irrelevant to the learning under consideration, they can be dropped at this point, and the situation evolves as portrayed in Figure 1.5.

In respect to the principles of the hierarchy of the sciences, the concept of mediation is the theory of primary importance from behavioristic psychology for social psychology. It is important because it provides a bridge between hypothetical constructs such as attitudes, values, prejudice, stereotypes, and so forth, and the central nervous system. The mediating response (rm-sm) carries two important implications: first, that the behavior is learned, and follows the laws of conditioning, and second, that the behavior is a product of the brain functioning. In other words, behaviors that the social psychologist labels attitudes, values, prejudice, steereotypes, and so forth, do not develop in some mysterious manner. These hypothetical constructs refer to meanings that are learned after being selected and then reinforced by the society in which the individual lives.

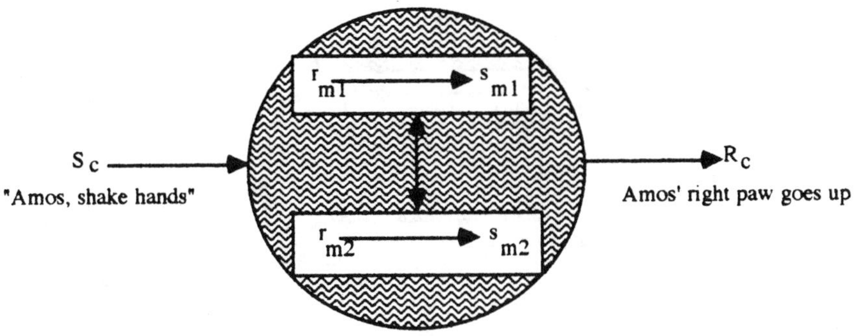

Figure 1.5

2. Symboling

Learning the words of a language is the cultural experience *par excellence*. No child has ever been born with the ability to speak a word. The child must learn the words of her language from others who already speak the language. Although there is a vast difference between the language abilities of Amos and any biologically normal three-year-old, the fundamental difference is not in their ability to be conditioned because they both follow, in the process of learning, the same law of conditioning. The difference between them lies in how far they can carry on the conditioning process and in how many times the conditioning process can be repeated, adding different Scs to the process.

Let's start where the child and Amos are at the same level, the ability to learn, that is, to follow the law of conditioning. Figures 1.6 and 1.7 show how the child learns the word "horse" (Osgood, Suci, & Tannenbaum, 1957, pp. 3–10).

We see in Figure 1.6 that for the child the process of learning the word "horse" is exactly the same as that for Amos learning "Amos, shake hands." Figure 1.7 shows only the encoding process involved, which is the meaning that the child attaches to the word "horse."

It is at the next level of conditioning that Amos and the child start to part ways, and where the Rubicon between humans and other animals begins. The child can continue to add meanings to environmental stimuli, whereas other animals are limited in this capacity. For example, if a three-year-old child knows the

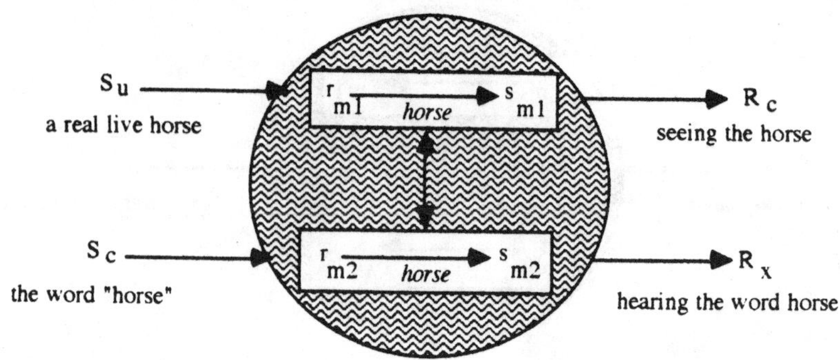

Figure 1.6

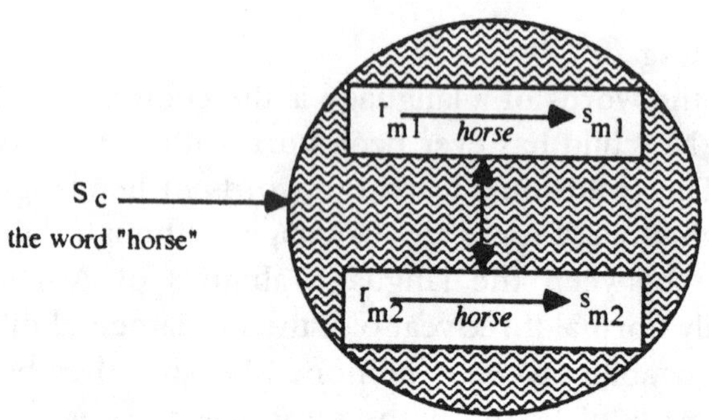

Figure 1.7

meanings of the words "horse," "black," "white " and "stripes," I can teach the child what a zebra is by saying "A zebra is a horse with black and white stripes," as portrayed in Figure 1.8.

Furthermore, we can continue to assign additional meanings to zebra, as long as the child already has the appropriate meanings. If the child doesn't have a particular meaning we want her to associate with "zebra'" (for example Africa), we can teach her the meaning of Africa and then say "zebras live in Africa." Most of the words in an adult's vocabulary are words to which such meanings have been assigned. No animal except humans has this abstracting ability.

The ability to proliferate symbols with any assigned arbitrary meaning whatsoever is a distinctly human ability, which the anthropologist Leslie White (1959) labels "symboling."

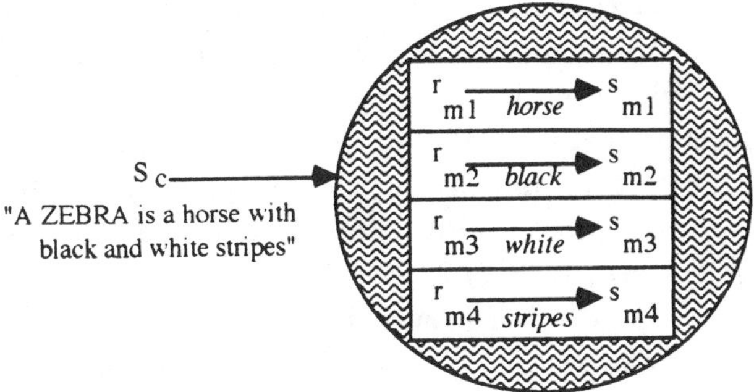

Figure 1.8

> By 'symboling' we mean bestowing meaning upon a thing or an act, or grasping and appreciating meaning thus bestowed. Holy water is a good example of such meanings. It is a human being who bestows the attribute of holiness on the water, and it may be comprehended and appreciated by other human beings. Articulate speech is the most characteristic and important form of symboling. Symboling is trafficking in nonsensory meanings. These nonsensory meanings, like the holiness of sacramental water, cannot be comprehended with the senses alone. Symboling is a kind of behavior. Only [humans are] capable of symboling. (p. 228)

There is, however, a downside to symboling, which occurs when we are not conscious of the fact that the symbol is not the thing for which it stands. As the field of general semantics points out, humans live in two worlds. There is the extensional world of things and events that we know firsthand. These are what we ourselves have seen, heard, smelled, or touched. Then there is the intensional world, which is the world created for us by our cultures. The world of symbols, for example the meanings of words that are found in dictionaries, may or may not be in correspondence with the real, extensional world. In the terminology of general semantics, it is here that the *map* (symbols, words) often does not accurately reflect the *territory* (the real world). ". . . [N]o matter how beautiful a map may be, it is useless to a traveler unless it accurately shows the relationship of places to each other . . . No harm will be done *unless someone tries to plan a trip by such a map* " (Hayakawa, 1978, p. 27, emphasis in the original).

A word that refers to something that cannot be seen, heard, smelled, or touched, has no extensional meaning. Scientific discourse rules out these types of words because there is no way, directly or indirectly, to verify their meaning with the senses. They are, however, very frequent in non-scientific discourse. Sometimes when the topic of conversation is an intensional word, the conversation can be fun, e.g., when one talks about 'dragons.' However, if the topic of conversation is a concept such as 'angels,' which has no extensional meaning whatsoever, the conversation can be endless, at best, or lead to conflict, at worst. Arguments about both 'dragons' and 'angels' are nonsense (non-sense) arguments because there is no way to detect the presence of either with the senses.

3. Abstracting

The first step in the process of symboling is the assignment of names to tangible things and events. As we discussed the preceding section, a name is an arbitrary sign that we attach to and use as a substitute for things and events that we come into contact with in our physical and social environment. Figure 1.9 traces another meaning process, even more distinctly a human process than symboling. In Figure 1.9, "Bessie" gets associated with a tangible cow following the same laws of conditioning described earlier for Amos learning to raise his paw to "shake," and the little girl learning the meaning of "zebra."

"Bessie" is a unique creature. No two events in nature are ever exactly alike (100% the same), and so it is that Bessie is like no other existing creature. Bessie does, however, resemble some other creatures; her shape and function are two such resemblances. It is on the basis of the common resemblances that we group Bessie with other creatures that we classify as 'cow.' The name 'cow' is, then, somewhat different from the name "Bessie." We associate "Bessie" with the tangible creature directly, whereas we associate 'cow' with real cows indirectly through the classification process. We call this procedure of grouping many instances of different events or items on the basis of some common but specific features *abstracting*.

The name "Bessie," since it is not the real extensional thing, leaves out many characteristics of the real Bessie, and is by this

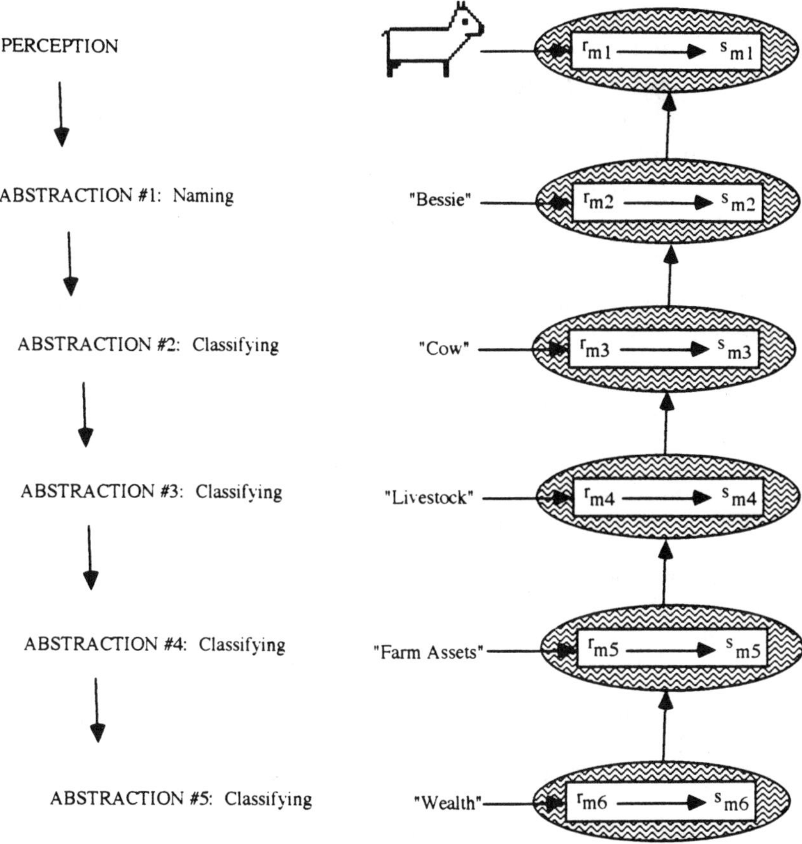

Figure 1.9

definition a type of abstraction. However, it is an extremely low level of abstraction because it is directly tied to the actual perception. 'Cow' is a higher level of abstraction since many of the characteristics peculiar to specific cows are not included in its meaning. In this manner we proceed up the abstraction ladder as shown in Figure 1.9. 'Cows' is classified as 'livestock,' which is classified as 'farm assets,' which is classified as 'wealth.'

The classification 'wealth' is at an extremely high level of abstraction since it omits all reference to any extensional characteristics of Bessie the cow. At every step going up the ladder of abstraction we have left out references to objective characteristics. When we classify "Bessie" as 'wealth,' we omit all reference to any tangible aspect of Bessie.

Abstracting at high levels is of course the unique feature of human culture. It allows a level of prediction and control of both the subjective and objective environments that is not the purview of any other animal. However, as with symboling, there is a downside to abstracting. We are unconscious of the fact that our classifications are simply a reflection of social convenience and necessity and that different necessities produce different classifications. Hayakawa (1978, pp. 160-161) gives an example of a meaningless type of thinking that is the result of never leaving the higher levels of abstraction (the intensional world).

> "What do you mean by *democracy*?"
> "Democracy means the preservation of human rights."
> "What do you mean by *rights*?"
> "By rights I mean those privileges God grants to all of us-I mean man's [sic] inherent privileges."
> "Such as?"
> "Liberty, for example."
> "What do you mean by *liberty*?"
> "Religious and political freedom."
> "And what does that mean?"
> "Religious and political freedom is what we enjoy under a democracy."

The major problem here is that the interlocutors are running around in verbal circles, and are completely unconscious of the mental operations involved. This lack of awareness can become especially frustrating, for both the speaker and the listener, if they think these words represent some kind of 'truth.' The way to avoid running around in verbal circles is to go down the abstraction ladder to the extensional world. For instance, in our homely example of Bessie the cow, it may in some circumstances be quite illuminating to ponder the fact that she may be 'wealth' to the stockyard owner but "Bessie" to the farmer who raised her.

C. Consciousness

1. A definition

An experiment that illustrates the effect of a mediating process of which we are not aware was one in which subjects were instructed to look at an apparently blank screen. However, on the screen a geometrical figure was flashed at very low illumination. It was so dim that the subjects were unaware that anything was on the screen. Following this 'blank' experience the subjects were asked to solve a problem that involved the use of the same geometrical figure that had been projected on the screen. The subjects proceeded to solve the problem totally unaware that they were making use of the mediating process that had been established subliminally. This is an example of behavior that is unconscious.

Another classic demonstration of the influence of mediating processes that are unconscious is a little experiment that you can conduct yourself. Write the roman numeral IX on a piece of paper, show it to a friend and then ask him or her what it is. The ordinary answer will be "nine." Now ask your friend to add one symbol and change the nine to a six. Many people who are otherwise competent in math cannot solve this simple problem. The point is that while trying to solve the problem they are unconscious of the fact that they have attached a particular meaning to the IX that is impeding their ability to find the solution. The same impediment I tried to establish in you by establishing the mental set for "roman numeral."

There is no question that much, if not a major part, of our behavior is unconscious, and it was the great contribution of Sigmund Freud to make us conscious of this fact. In psychoanalytic (i.e., Freudian) terms, 'unconscious' is also used to describe behavior where individuals, in addition to not being able to describe their mental state, will, if one is suggested, deny or oppose the suggestion that this is in fact the case.

An important aspect of Freud's account of unconscious thinking is his description of the ego-defense mechanisms that we all employ to guard our self-esteem. There are occasions when each of us suffers from feelings of inferiority, guilt, insecurity, and being unloved. Freud discovered that at these times we often engage unconsciously in strategies like repression and rationalization to protect our pride and self-esteem. In repression we will permit no outlet for any unpleasant wish or thought, and in rationalization we develop 'good' reasons to justify our misdeeds.

It is noteworthy that there is nothing abnormal or 'sick' in the use of a defense mechanism. All normal persons employ them in their adjustment to the storm and stress of everyday life. The defense mechanisms become neurotic behavior when they are the only or main way an individual adjusts to life's problems.

> It is not the value which attaches to the act nor its frequency or rarity that determines whether the act is healthy or neurotic. Whether any act is healthy or neurotic depends only on the nature of the constellation of forces which determines it. If those forces . . . are of such a nature that they predetermine the automatic repetition of the act, irrespective of any considerations, then that act can be considered a neurotic act. (Kubie as cited in Allport, 1961, p. 152)

It is important to note, contrary to popular belief, that responses that are the result of mediation processes of which the person is not conscious are not qualitatively different from conscious ones. There is no basis for suspecting them to be nefarious, primitive, ugly, evil, dirty, or such. To say that we do something and cannot give a verbal account of why is not the same thing as saying we did it because of a questionable motive.

When individuals are aware of their inner feelings, their private reactions, their perception of the physical world, their ego defenses, they are 'conscious.' In the present discussion the term 'awareness' is used synonymously with the term 'consciousness.' In both cases the operating principle is that these two words are operationally defined in terms of language. If persons can give a verbal account of their mental state they are said to be conscious. At the other extreme, if they are unable to give any verbal account of the mental state associated with their behavior, the persons are said to be 'unconscious' of that behavior. In terms of our previous discussion, 'consciousness' is awareness of the mediational process that intervenes between an objective or subjective stimulus and an objective or subjective response. The sign of consciousness is the individual's ability to put into words the mediating process; The greater the ability to verbalize the mental state, the greater the consciousness.

2. Unconscious Sign Behavior

As indicated above, the major part of our behavior is unconscious. Tomorrow morning put the spotlight of consciousness on your behavior while you are getting dressed. Put into words, every move that you make. You will realize from this little exercise how much you do unconsciously in just a brief period, and by extrapolation you can understand the basis of the statement that a major part of our daily behavior is unconscious.

If this is true of your behavior in general, it is also true of your speech sign behavior, in particular. The large majority of the speech signs you emit are unconscious. Of the many ramifications of this aspect of speech sign behavior, two that are most important for an understanding of how the unconscious operates in the case of speech signs are immanent reference and psychic determinism (Pittenger, Hockett, & Danehy, 1960).

Immanent reference refers to the fact that no matter what else you are talking about, or think you are talking about, you are always talking about the context in which your talking is taking place. The context includes your own physical and mental state, your attitudes toward the person you are talking to, and your attitudes toward the physical environment in which the conversation is taking place. The word "talking" in the preceding sentences refers not only to the linguistic signs, but also to paralinguistic signs. You can, for instance say, "I *like* what you're saying." However, while uttering these words you may unconsciously emit paralinguistic behavior that indicates "I *don't like* what you're saying." In one way or another, our observable behavior indicates our thoughts about the here-and-now.

We often overlook immanent reference because of our ability to talk about the not-here-and-not-now. The vast majority of our conversations are about things and events that are not present to our senses. Linguists label this type of behavior 'displaced speech,' and the procedure is the same as the one described above when the child learned that "A zebra is a horse with black and white stripes that lives in Africa." While I was talking to the child about zebras in Africa, neither of which was present at the time, I was communicating to her what my mental state was; e.g., that I was having a pleasant time teaching her about zebras and Africa. She was communicating to me her mental state, e.g., that she was enjoying my teaching her these things.

The practical implication of the principle of immanent reference is that we should always be prepared to ask to what extent and in what way the behavior of people talking to us is an index of emotions and attitudes not being expressed overtly in the words that they are uttering. The question is not always easily answered, but if it is not asked we can never have the answer.

The second principle, 'psychic determinism,' is closely related to the concept of the unconscious, and it also comes to us through the writings of Freud. In essence, 'psychic determinism' means that every behavioral response is related to a mediating process.

> This notion holds that the behavior of a single individual is not to any significant extent determined by his [/her] own ingenuity and inventiveness, nor by his [/her] genetic character, although obviously the latter factor plays at least a limit-setting role. The major determinants are held to be the behavioral patterns transmitted to the individual by enculturation from those around him [/her] in the same community. Individual inventiveness is not denied, but it is regarded as a matter of recombination of separately-acquired cultural patterns. (Pittenger et al., 1960, p. 232)

One implication of this principle is that "nothing never happens." No response to "can you help me?" is a nothing that is a something, a significant and important something.

Another implication of this principle is that there is no such thing as an accidental speech sign. The speaker may be sorry and not have intended to utter a particular word, but that unintended act has a cause and it is related to some mental state. "We can only profitably assume that people may not always say what they mean, but they always mean what they say. As with immanent reference, the value of this aphorism is that it informs us to ask questions, to be alert in a certain way, that we might otherwise not be" (Pittenger et al., 1960, p. 254).

3. Consciousness Raising

Because an interlocutor is always communicating about the here-and-now (immanent reference), and because there is no such thing as a communication accident (psychic determinism), it is possible to know what is on the 'mind' of those who are talking to you. Also, in your responses, it is possible to know what's on your mind. These are the implications of the preceding discussion.

> The only way we can know anything of the "mind" of another person is through observation of, and inference from, his [/her] communicative behavior. . . . Communicative behavior is the external reality that we can jointly observe and discuss and sometimes agree about.
>
> We can say that we know the 'mind' of another person, practically speaking, only to the extent that we are familiar with his [/her] communicative habits and can predict how he [/she] will react communicatively to the various types of situation in which he [/she] is apt to find him[/her] self.
>
> Similarly, a person can say that he [/she] knows his [/her] own "mind," practically speaking, only in the same way-only to the extent that he [/she] is familiar with his [/her] own communicative habits and can predict how he [/she] will react communicatively to the various types of situation in which he [/she] is apt to find him [/her] self. . . . For all practical purposes, then, the "mind" of a person is the same thing as the totality of his [/her] communicative habits. (Pittenger et al., 1960, pp. 246–247)

If people you know intend to cause you physical harm, it is very likely that in your conversations with them they will have emitted linguistic and paralinguistic signs that indicate that this is their intention. It is not by some mysterious power that you can discern their intention. It is simply accomplished by bringing fully into consciousness what you think about the behavior that you are perceiving at the moment. It is the same method invoked when you became conscious of your behavior while getting dressed in the exercise above: by expressing in words what you are thinking.

The man who attacks a woman he knows, has probably emitted linguistic and paralinguistic signs that were clues to the subsequent attack. Sexist speech signs were present and perceived by the unfortunate woman, but she never really asked herself: "What do I feel like when he uses sexist words or condescending voice qualities?" If this question is not asked, it can't be answered. If it is asked, and the answer is "not good," the woman has a powerful bit of information in that she knows what is on the mind of the man.

The man also can, by putting the spotlight of his consciousness on the same behavior, become conscious of his sexist words or condescending voice qualities. He can ask himself the question "What are my intentions when I do these things? Would I talk like this with my mother? My sister?"

Both the woman and the man, armed with the knowledge that comes from consciousness raising, now have the potential to act rationally. Aware of the fact that their speech sign behavior is an expression of their values, they now have a choice: if the behavior does not accurately reflect their values, they have the choice of talking in a manner that does.

2

Emotive States: I

A. Perception

1. Definition

Every stimulus arriving at the brain has a meaning attached to it. When a human responds to a stimulus it is most often impossible to tell what was the exact sensory stimulation to which the person is responding. This is a result of the fact that when the afferent nervous system delivers a message from a sensory receptor to the brain, all the conditioned responses associated with that stimulus are called forth. This operation proceeds in exceedingly rapid manner. The term 'perception' refers to this process. Perception is sensory stimulation plus meaning. In a manner of speaking, it is 'social sensation.'

The 'mental teaser' in Chapter 1 is an illustration of the transformation of sensory experiences into perceptual meanings. When you saw the IX preceded by the words "roman numeral" you perceived it as 'nine.' However, the same two symbols appear in the word 'SIX.' In both cases the sensory experience was exactly the same, but your perceptual experience is quite different as a function of the mental set 'roman numeral' in one case, and 'arabic numeral' in the other.

The specific contribution of social psychology to the study of human behavior is the focus on the importance of culture and personality in understanding the human thought process (Klineberg, 1954). One definition of culture is that it is the set of ready-made answers to all the common problems of life provided by the society in which an individual is reared. When a society has conditioned its members with these ready-made answers, their perception then conforms to cultural standards. Anthropologists are a source of many examples of this phenomenon: a chieftain from Swaziland sees all London traffic officers as extremely friendly because in his country an upraised arm is a warm greeting; in India a physician who says "the patient will recover" is highly respected and revered, in Chile a physician making the same statement will be considered arrogant and not to be trusted; and so on (Allport, 1961).

Personal perception refers to the screening of incoming stimulation. This screening is a function of a person's emotions and attitudes when the sensory stimulation arrives at the central nervous system. This does not imply that his or her experience is unique and not cultural. Quite the contrary, individuals can only associate meanings to stimuli that have been taught to them by their culture. "Personal," in this case, means responding in terms of one of the several alternatives or ready-made answers provided by enculturation. Many experiments have demonstrated the role of personal factors in perception: students who rate themselves as being pessimistic and distrustful will recall more gloomy-sounding words than students who rate themselves as being optimistic and trusting; coins are perceived as larger than cardboard disks the same size; hungry people will perceive ink-blots as hamburgers; and so on (Allport, 1961).

The ready-made classification of things and events allows us to cope with the millions of stimuli that bombard our senses. Perception organizes our sensory input such that we don't have to start every day building up new classifications of our daily experiences. Anyone who has experienced going from his or her own to a significantly different culture can verify the wrenching experience of *culture shock.* Culture shock stems primarily from either an inability to associate appropriate meanings to new and novel stimuli, or relatively familiar stimuli appearing in an entirely different context. Serious problems may arise when an individual's perception of a thing or event extensionally existing is a misinterpretation or representation of the thing or event's actual nature. Such illusions may be deceptive or misleading. In most cases a deceptive or misleading perception is harmless. For example, employing an optical illusion in a fun-house or using the stereotype of physicians being males in a riddle the solution to which depends on perceiving the physician as being a female. However, illusions and stereotypes can have quite serious effects when they operate in a situation where a true response, rather than an illusionary one, is necessary to cope with the real, extensional world.

2. Illusions

An impressive demonstration of the law of conditioning on human perception that is also an outstanding example of completely unconscious behavior, was a research project by Segall, Campbell, and Herskovits (1966) *The Influence of Culture on Visual Perception*. Two of the several optical illusions employed in their research were the Sander parallelogram illusion and the Muller-Lyer illusion that are shown in Figures 2.1 and 2.2.

For both illusions the question to be answered is "Which line is longer, 'a' or 'b'?" If you check reality, in this case by measuring the lettered lines in each of the illusions, you will have demonstrated to yourself the effects of deceptive or misleading perception. However, the most astonishing aspect of the Segall, Campbell, and Herskovits study is that not everyone is deceived or misled by this illusion–it does not hold up cross-culturally! These illusions were shown to people in the U.S.A. and in Africa, and it was discovered that Africans did not fall for the illusion. The Africans saw the reality that the lines with the

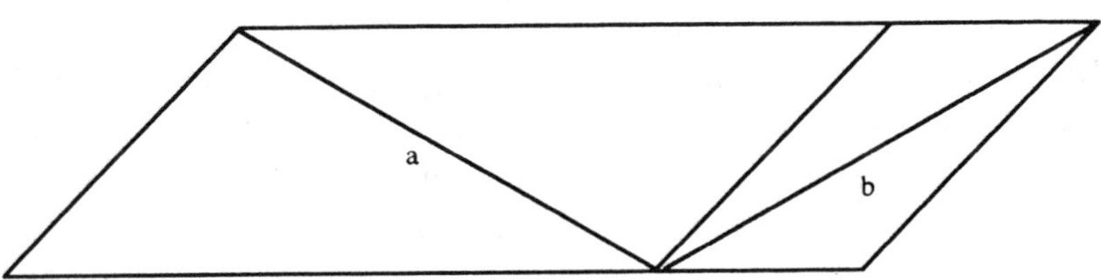

Figure 2.1: The Sander parallelogram illusion

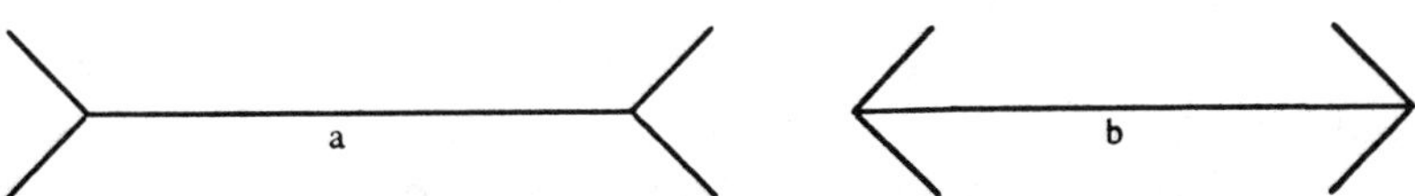

Figure 2.2: The Muller-Lyer illusion

letter 'a' in both illusions are equal in length to the lines with the letter 'b.' The authors explain these results in terms of the *Carpentered World Hypothesis*.

> Our version of this hypothesis can best be described by applying it to the Sander parallelogram. . . . For this drawing, the well-established tendency-at least of Western or Westernized respondents-is to judge the diagonal on the respondent's left as longer than it really is. This bias is understandable if one perceives a nonorthogonal parallelogram drawn on a flat surface as the representation of a rectangular surface extended in space. Given such a tendency, it is clear that the represented *distance* covered by the left diagonal is greater than the represented distance covered by the right diagonal.
>
> A tendency such as this constitutes a habit of inference that has great ecological validity–and great functional utility–in highly carpentered environments. Western societies provide environments replete with rectangular objects; these objects, when projected on the retina, are represented by non-rectangular images. For people living in carpentered worlds, the tendency to interpret obtuse and acute angles in retinal images as deriving from rectangular objects is likely to be so pervasively reinforced that it becomes automatic and unconscious relatively early in life. For those living where . . . [construction is] . . . without benefit of carpenters' tools (saw, plane, straight edge, tape measure, carpenter's square, spirit level, plumb bob, chalk line, surveyor's sight, etc.) straight lines and precise right angles are a rarity. As a result, the inference habit of interpreting acute and obtuse angles as right angles extended in space would not be learned, at least not as well. (p. 84)

It has also been amply demonstrated that such illusions not only influence the perception of our physical environment, but they are also a pervasive aspect of the perception of social behavior. One experiment (Klineberg, 1954, p. 211) demonstrated that the perception of a 'correct' or 'incorrect' performance of a particular behavior by an individual is a function of the perceiver's attitude towards the individual performing this behavior. In a classroom situation, an experimenter identified students who were liked by all the students in the class and those who were disliked by all the students in the class. Outside the classroom she instructed the liked students on how to perform a particular series of calisthenic exercises incorrectly, and an equal number of disliked students to perform exactly the same calisthenic exercises correctly. She then had the two groups perform the exercises in front of their classmates. When they had completed the exercises, the experimenter asked the class to vote on which one of the two groups had done the exercises correctly. The result was that a majority of the votes went to the liked group. In conversations with the students afterwards, the experimenter reported that she believed that the students saw the differences that were the basis of their votes. In this case it was not the physical environment that had conditioned a false perception, it was the mental environment. It was the attitudes of the perceivers that caused them to be completely misled in their perception of reality. This experiment, and many others like it, support the conclusion that a person's mental set toward others is the major factor in determining how they perceive that person's behavior, and that particular mental sets can result is an illusionary response to reality.

3. Stereotypes

A stereotype is a mental set to respond in a categorical manner towards a group of people (Hollander, 1976, p. 155). Such a group of people has at least one distinctive feature that all members of the group share, e.g., size of nose, physique, hair style, and so forth. It is a characteristic of stereotypes that any individual manifesting the identifying distinctive feature is perceived in terms of the category that has been associated with that distinctive feature. This is the illusionary aspect of stereotypes: basing perception on an abstract category and not the real person. Several research studies have demonstrated experimentally the ability of stereotypes to create gross distortions of reality. In one such study, photographs of thirty young women were shown to a group of college students. These students then rated the photographs in terms of several personality characteristics: general liking, beauty, intelligence, character, and so forth. Several months later the same students were shown exactly the same photographs but this time with family names added. The names added to the photographs were selected because of their distinctiveness and association with certain ethnic groups: Rabinowitz and Finklestein with Jews; Scarano and Grisolia with Italians; McGillicuddy and O'Shaughnessy with Irish; Adams and Clark with 'old American.' The students then rated the same thirty photographs a second time with these names added. The ratings changed dramatically. The

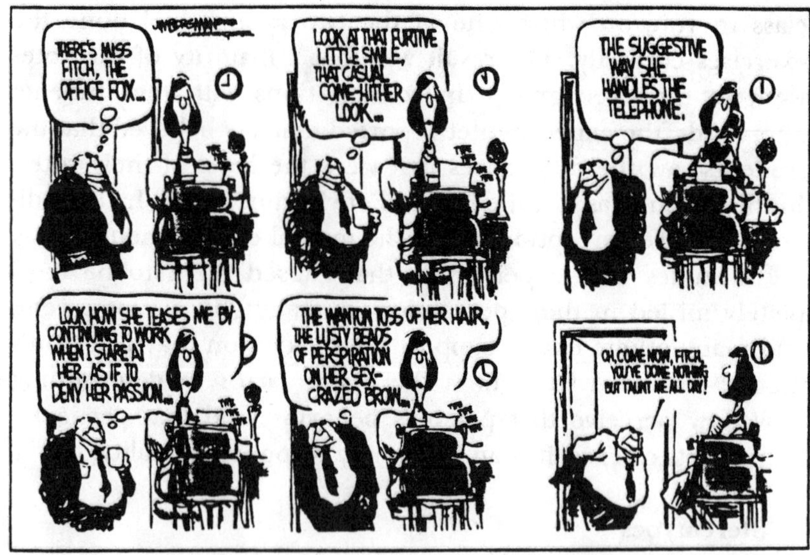

Phyllis Schlafly, anti-ERA spokesperson, took the curious position that working women had themselves to blame for sexual harassment in the office.

Figure 2.3

addition of Jewish and Italian names resulted in a significant increase in negative ratings. These college students perceived several photographs without names as "I like her," with the addition of Jewish or Italian names, the perception became "I don't like her" (Klineberg, 1954, p. 211).

In U.S. culture the most pervasive distortions of reality are a result of stereotypes of black people and women. For example, to examine the effect on perception of the stereotype that whites in the U.S. have of blacks, researchers presented a picture of an attractive house with very nicely landscaped grounds to a group of White children and asked "What is the black woman doing?" Most of them replied that she was cleaning up the house. However, there was no black woman in the picture! The cartoon above (Figure 2.3) illustrates the effect on perception of the stereotype that men in the U.S. have of women.[1]

B. Attitudes

1. Definition

Illusions and stereotypes are relatively permanent mental sets to respond in a certain way to a stimulus when the particular extensional stimulus is present. It is the actual looking at the Sander parallelogram or the female secretary that calls forth the illusion in the viewers. An attitude, like a perception, is a relatively permanent predisposition to respond in a certain way, but in the case of an attitude the object of reference does not have to be tangibly present for the mental set to be called forth. This is a fine distinction from one point of view, but the differentiation of mental sets into perceptions and attitudes defines a major difference between experimental and social psychology: "The concept of attitude has for a long time been the mainstay or working tool of the social psychologist" (Bugelski, 1960, p. 337); and "attitude has to do with people's orientation to definite facets of the environment (including people, culture and society) it is the favored concept in social psychology" (Allport, 1961, p. 348).

Attitudes are a category of sign behavior and follow the laws of conditioning as described in the preceding chapter. Figure 2.4 shows the development of an attitude as a mediating process. 'Unpleasant' is the attitudinal part of the mental set in

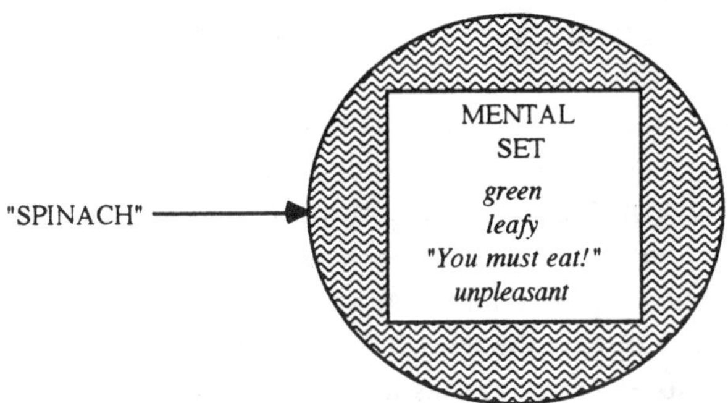

Figure 2.4

response to spinach. For some people, merely the word 'spinach' is sufficient to arouse this negative attitude.

Just as perception is at the interstices of experimental and social psychology, attitudes are at the interstices of social psychology and anthropology. *Ideology* is an anthropological concept, and it includes in its definition the concept of 'attitude.' In the following definition of ideology, '*opinions*' and '*values*' are terms referring to types and categories of attitudes.

> Each of us knows that our own external behavior is preceded, accompanied, and followed by a ceaseless stream of mental and emotional experiences. . . . Although these cognitive and emotional events and their verbal or other manifestations appear to originate in each individual's private inner being, it is a fundamental principle of anthropological analysis that most if not all of this inner behavior and its overt expression conform to definite culturally determined patterns, which originate outside the individual. Ideology thus embraces the entire realm of socially patterned thought. It includes the explicit and implicit knowledge, opinions, values, plans, and goals that people have about their ecological circumstances. (Harris, 1975, p. 158)

The concept of attitude implies a mental set towards something, and most often it is the 'pro' or 'con' aspect of a particular value. It is the extensional way we know that individuals hold particular values; they approve or disapprove of certain political beliefs, they like or dislike certain religious ceremonies, they approach or avoid certain people, and so forth. This approach-avoidance aspect of attitudes implies a motor response to a stimulus, not only a mental one. There is a linking of the possibility of physical action to the concept 'attitude' that is not linked to the concepts 'perception' or 'ideology.' An attitude prepares a person to perform a particular behavior, even though the behavior may not take place.

We learn attitudes as a result of several different types of experiential conditions. One condition that leads to an attitude is the frequent association of a particular object, person or event, or with a particular type of situation. An example would be a young white child who has never seen a black woman in any other situation except as a domestic worker, could develop the attitude that all black women are domestic servants; a male who has seen numerous movie and T.V. demonstrations of women melting at the mere gaze of a male, may develop the attitude that merely looking at a woman will bring on an uncontrollable desire for him on her part.

Another major condition for the formation of a particular attitude is a traumatic or dramatic experience associated with the object. A woman that has been assaulted by a man may develop a 'hostile' or 'avoidance' attitude towards all men. On the other hand, a woman that has had an extremely positive experience with a man could develop a 'friendly' (or 'approach') attitude towards men.

Most attitudes, however, are ready-made answers supplied by parents, friends, and teachers. This type of mental set depends less on individual experience and more on accepting the viewpoints of significant others in the social environment. The most important function of socialization is to teach children the attitudes of the culture in which they live. Whether this is done formally, by saying to the child "you do this, not this," or informally, as when the child imitates adult behavior, the child is conditioned to have the attitudes of his/her community. This process has been studied by learning psychologists and is called "secondary reinforcement" (Hollander, 1976, p. 118). The primary conditioning factor in secondary reinforcement is parental approval. Children learn the attitudes of their parents because they want their love and affection. The reason, when as adults we find it so difficult to raise our consciousness about certain unpleasant or disconcerting attitudes, is that these attitudes have been taught to us by people we admire and love.

2. Prejudice[2]

A prejudice is a type of attitude. The unique characteristic of a prejudice is that it is a prejudgment for or against a group of people. Prejudices are evaluative responses not based on actual experience. They are mental sets that involve very strong emotional responses to things not immanently present. The essential difference between a stereotype and a prejudice is that a stereotype exists in the extensional world of sensation, whereas a prejudice exists in the intensional world of abstractions, i.e., words. As a result it is relatively easy to raise one's consciousness about a stereotype and extremely difficult to raise one's consciousness about a prejudice. For example, it is possible to present to a person who maintains a stereotype of Jews that involves the mental set that the distinctive features of Jews are black hair, brown eyes, and long straight noses with evidence, say photographs, that show Jews who are blond, blue-eyed, and who have small upturned noses. The persons with false impressions of the distinctive features of Jews can then adjust their mental map to reflect accurately the real world. However, those who harbor a prejudice toward Jews do not base their highly emotional responses on the behavior of Jews for which there is extensional evidence. Anti-Semites have difficulty in identifying any distinctive features of Jews, and often have to fall back on arguments like "childlike intuition" to prove their point. An example of such an anti-Semitic argument is the following:

> Very small children, especially girls, frequently have a quite marked instinct for race. It frequently happens that children who have no conception of what 'Jew' means, or that there is such a thing in the world, begin to cry as soon as a genuine Jew or Jewess comes near them. The learned frequently cannot tell a Jew from a non-Jew; a child that scarcely knows how to speak notices the difference. (Klineberg, 1954, p. 513)

If an attitude is erroneous, misleading, or deceptive, the cause of an illusionary response to certain groups of people, it is a special kind of attitude, it is a prejudice.

A primary component of *sexism,* for example, is a prejudice in which superiority or inferiority, unsupported by any evidence, in traits, abilities, social value, personal worth, is associated with males or females as a group (Albee, 1981). There is much experimental evidence that indicates that in U.S. culture children, men, and women believe negative personality characteristics are associated with women, whereas positive characteristics are associated with men. One investigation asked a large number of men and women to rate the personality characteristics of men and women. The results indicated that males were rated as independent, objective, active, competitive, logical, adventurous, and self-confident and on the same scales women were rated in the opposite direction. Men are rated as competent and women as incompetent. Women are rated as gentle, sensitive to the feelings of others, tactful, neat, quiet, and interested in art and literature, and men as possessing the opposite traits. In other words, women are prejudged to be 'warm and expressive' whereas men are 'cold and inexpressive.' These prejudices are unfortunate and harmful to the personalities of the men and women who hold these prejudices. For men, the primary harm of sexism is that they come to feel that they must always be competent, always appear strong and tough and not to express their feelings. Thus, they stifle their own personal development. For women there is the low self-esteem that becomes part of their personalities, developing at times into at least social and professional insecurity and frequently into a fear of success, when they incorporate the image of incompetence into the perception that they are incompetent. When they are successful, some women develop the *impostor syndrome,* a feeling that their success is a mistake and any minute they will be exposed as incompetent.

Like any attitude, a prejudice is learned. Children are not born racists or sexists, and there is no gene that creates these mental maps. The strongest evidence demonstrating the fact that prejudice is not natural comes from studies that show that racial prejudice is entirely absent in young children. As any native of the 'old South' will attest there were, in former times, intimate associations between black and white children until these relationships were prevented by parents or teachers. In one late thirties' investigation in a small town in Tennessee, it was discovered that not only did white and black children play together until it was forbidden to do so, these children tried to continue their friendships with each other in spite of parental opposition. Parents reported that they had to punish their children more than once before they learned the 'appropriate' behavior. In another classic sociometric study, young school children were asked to rate their classmates in terms of whom they would like to have sit next to them. There was no appearance of a preference for white or blacks to sit next to them until the third grade.

The good news is that since prejudices are learned they can also be unlearned. However, the unlearning process cannot begin unless we become aware of the fact that we are prejudiced. In other words, the first step in combating a prejudice is consciousness raising. If we become conscious of the fact that we are prejudiced against a certain group, it is then possible to concentrate on changing any false beliefs we have about that group. If we can respond to individuals not as a "black" or a "chick" but as "John" and "Jane," it is then possible to free ourselves of erroneous mental sets. It is impossible for white people who have been raised in U.S. culture not to have been reared with prejudices towards blacks, and for men in U.S. culture not to have been reared with prejudices towards women. However, just as knowledge of the fact that we live in a carpentered world leads us to measure the lines in optical illusions, if we are conscious that we also live in a racist and sexist world we can begin to free ourselves from the erroneous notions, illusions, and delusions these prejudices have created in our thinking and we can try to change.

3. Attitude Measurement

Psychology has its origins in the study of the relation between mental states and physical stimuli, which was termed the science of 'psychophysics.' In psychophysical experiments subjects would be presented with two stimuli and asked to judge whether they were the same or different. In this manner a *threshold* of stimulation was calculated and the amount of physical difference required for a mental difference was calculated. The *semantic differential* is a modern version of this classic psychophysical technique. Instead of weights, sounds or illumination, the typical stimuli in the classic experiments, the semantic differential employs familiar adjective pairs to observe attitudes associated with a stimulus. The underlying assumption of this procedure is that a native speaker of English has very precise and strong meanings associated with bipolar adjective pairs like good-bad, strong-weak, and fast-slow, that they have mental sets to respond to any stimulation in terms of the attitudes expressed in these adjective pairs, and that the semantic differential procedure provides a controlled method of bringing forth these associations.

In the following example the wording of the instructions is typical for a study in which the subjects are being asked for their attitudes towards people they hear on a tape recording.

The purpose of this study is to measure your *attitude* to people on the basis of hearing them on a tape recording. Here is how you are to use these scales:

If you feel that your attitude toward the person you hear speaking is *very closely related* to one end of the scale, you should place your check mark as follows:

fair _X_:___:___:___:___:___ unfair

or

fair ___:___:___:___:___:_X_ unfair

If you feel that your attitude toward the person you hear speaking is *quite closely related* to one or the other end of the scale (but not extremely), you should place your check mark as follows:

fair ___:_X_:___:___:___:___ unfair

or

fair ___:___:___:___:_X_:___ unfair

If you feel that your attitude toward the person you hear speaking is *only slightly related* to one or the other end of the scale, you should place your check mark as follows:

fair ___:___:_X_:___:___:___ unfair

or

fair ___:___:___:_X_:___:___ unfair

IMPORTANT: (1) Place your check-marks in the middle of spaces, not on the boundaries:

this · not this

fair ___:___:_X_:___:___:X___ unfair

(2) Do not put more than one check mark on a single scale.

As the result of many investigations of having subjects describe their attitudes in terms of these bipolar adjective scales towards all sorts of things and events, Osgood and his colleagues (1957) discovered that any attitude can be described in terms of three dimensions that they labeled evaluative, potency, and activity. The primary bipolar adjective scales that represent the evaluative dimension are: good-bad, nice-awful, pleasant-unpleasant; the potency dimension: strong-weak, large-small, heavy-light; and the activity dimension: fast-slow, active-passive, sharp-dull. The mean of subjects' ratings on the three adjective pairs representing a particular dimension represents their mental set for that dimension. The important implications of the semantic differential research are that if you have an individual tell you his/her attitude toward a particular stimulus in terms of bipolar adjective scales representing these three dimensions, you will know almost all there is to know about his/her attitude toward that stimulus; and second, when a speaker uses any one of these adjectives or their synonyms to describe a person, place, or thing, it is an index of his/her attitude towards that person, place, or thing. Finally, the use of an adverbial qualification of the adjective, for example, 'extremely fair' or 'quite fair,' or no adverbial qualification at all, for example, 'fair,' indicates the strength of that attitude.

C. Observing Attitudes

1. Situations

As indicated above, an attitude is a relatively permanent predisposition to respond to a particular stimulus. Reversing this proposition: a behavioral response is the overt manifestation of a particular attitude. We come to know a person's personality by observing his/her behavioral responses. However, we never encounter an individual apart from a particular context, and it is context that determines which particular attitude is activated (Allport, 1961, pp. 174–181). People have many attitudes, some of them contradictory, and the attitude that is called forth at a given moment is a function of how individuals perceive a given situation in which they find themselves. For example, one investigator developed a questionnaire regarding attitudes toward religious doctrines. One series of questions started with the question "As a member of *your church* how do you feel about ______?" In another series the questions started with "How do you *personally* feel about ______?" The same content was supplied in the blank spaces (e.g., drinking alcohol). It was found that the same respondent would give opposite answers depending on how the question was phrased. It is noteworthy that the expression of contradictory attitudes does not necessarily mean that the person is lying or being hypocritical. What it does demonstrate is that personality is multifaceted, and that individuals have complex systems of attitudes any one of which may be evoked by the physical, social, or cultural situation in which they find themselves. Finally, according to Allport, what a person will do in any given situation is the result of at least four conditions: (1) enduring personality characteristics; (2) defense mechanisms; (3) the relevance of the situation to the ego; and (4) the behavior expected (p. 180).

Given these considerations, it can be seen that a central problem for social psychologists who study attitudes are the physical, social, or cultural characteristics of the situation in which they gather their data. If their results are to yield a valid portrayal of their subjects' attitudes, the behavior observed has to be typical or natural. No social psychologist studying attitudes believes that his/her methods produce behavior on the part of his/her subjects that is completely natural. However, over the years several methods of *conduct sampling* have been employed for the systematic observation of personal behavior (Allport, 1961, p. 414). These techniques try to put the subject in a situation that will produce behavior that, although not exactly the same, is highly similar to the behavior the subject performs in every day life situations and which accurately reflect the subject's attitudes. The primary techniques that are employed to accomplish this are the miniature real life situation and the interview.

2. The Miniature Real-Life Situation[3]

It is possible to create an 'experimental' situation that is so similar to real life that one can be confident that the results observed would hold true in real life. The flight trainers used in teaching pilots how to fly are an example. The student sits in a model of the cockpit of an airplane and operates it in situations that simulate real flying. On the basis of the student pilot's behavior, it is possible to make quite accurate predictions on her/his ability to fly a real airplane.

A very dramatic demonstration of the ability of miniature real life situations to observe attitudes toward stress and to predict future behavior in the presence of stress, was the work done in the OSS during World War II (as cited in Allport, 1961). One of the main tasks of the OSS assessment staff was to select individuals who would be dropped behind the lines in enemy territory. The candidates were brought to a secluded farm area in Virginia where they were given extensive batteries of psychological tests and participated in miniature real life situations structured by the assessment staff. In one such miniature real life exercise the candidate had to build a structure in 10 minutes with aid of two 'helpers.' Helpers is in quotations because they were confederates (stooges in everyday parlance) who were trained to act in ways to impede the candidate from accomplishing the assigned task. The assessment staff observed the candidate's behavior and reported on the attitude of the candidate to this stressful situation. After the war, the candidate's behavior in the miniature real life situation proved to be the single best predictor of success or failure in work behind enemy lines.

3. The Interview[4]

An interview is a type of conversation. It is an interchange of thoughts by means of spoken words in which one of the interlocutors seeks to have the other interlocutor communicate in speech information of a personal nature. Interviews provide a format for asking people about various topics in such a manner that they will reveal their attitudes in their responses. In one sense an interview is a miniature real life situation; however, it is a situation in which the specific aim is having the subject produce verbal behavior.

Whether an interview will produce verbal behavior that is a valid sample of the subject's typical responses depends on the interviewee's attraction to and comfort with the interviewer. A major factor that contributes to such interpersonal attraction and feelings of comfort is the similarity between the interviewer and the interviewee. For example, young black children are likely to produce invalid verbal responses, that is, responses that are not typical either of their verbal behavior or their attitudes, when the interviewer is an adult white male. The most accurate interviews occur when the interviewer and interviewee are of the same ethnic group and social class. If an interviewer is perceived to have some kind of power over the interviewee, it is unlikely that the interview will contain accurate indicators of emotions and attitudes. However, it is possible to reduce the apprehension of interviewees by increasing their attraction to and comfort with the interviewer. In other words, it is possible to reduce apprehension when the interviewee trusts the interviewer.

Another factor determining whether an interview will produce verbal behavior that is a valid sample of the subject's typical responses, is the extent to which the interviewee is prompted to produce responses that will please the interviewer. Rosenthal (1966, 1985) has provided ample evidence for the *experimenter effect,* which is the label for the condition of an interviewer's preconceived expectations causing a distortion in the responses produced by the interviewee. Rosenthal's work indicates that the distorting effect of communicating biases to interviewees cannot be minimized. Interviewers do not have to put into words what their biases are. Subtle nonverbal gestures can provide enough of a stimulus to direct the interviewee to communicate the desired response.

One method of avoiding the experimenter effect is the careful wording of the questions that are asked. There are special problems that have been identified in the wording of interview questions, and interviewers should avoid using language that results in these problems if they want valid responses. A wording of questions that should be avoided is one that suggests an answer to the interviewee. A question like "You do support The Equal Rights Amendment, don't you?" is a *leading question*; it is leading because it suggests an appropriate response. A second type of question to avoid is one that is worded so that it creates an attitude on the part of the interviewee when none exists. A question like "What do you think about Turks?" may produce a response pro or con, when the interviewee has never even heard of Turks. People do not like to appear indifferent or uninformed, and it is incumbent on the interviewer to indicate that it is appropriate for the interviewee to say that he/she does not know or understand what it is the interviewer is asking about.

Careful attention to the language and the complexity of interview questions can help avoid leading the interviewee to give certain responses or create an attitude when none exists, and at the same time, it can also help increase the attraction toward and the comfort with the interviewer. The questions themselves indicate to the interviewee the attitude of the interviewer towards them and may serve to increase their trust in the interviewer, and their willingness to give honest answers.

3

Emotive States: II

A. Interpersonal Orientation

1. Motivation

An individual's overall behavior is a pattern of many separate elements of behavior. That is, every person is the source and destination of hundreds of stimuli at the same instant all the time. A psychological theory can attempt to explain either the individual's overall pattern of behavior or it may concentrate on one or more of the separate elements that constitute the overall pattern. Similarly, psychological concepts may be labels for general patterns of behavior or they may be labels for specific types of behavior that occur in specific situations. A concept such as 'prejudice' is a label for a general pattern of behavior that occurs in response to stimuli that may be quite vague. 'Prejudice' is a label for the individual's behavior both as the source and the destination of varied and complex stimuli. On the other hand, a concept such as 'classical conditioning' refers to the behavior of the individual as the destination of stimuli. Classical conditioning only attempts to explain behavior that has occurred in response to a specific stimulus in a specific manner.

Psychological theories that attempt to explain overall patterns of behavior are personality theories while psychological theories that attempt to explain separate elements of behavior are 'single-domain' theories. Single-domain theories

> make no pretense at being a general theory of behavior and are content to develop concepts appropriate for the description and prediction of a limited array of behavioral events. Theories of personality, however, have generally accepted the challenge of accounting for or incorporating events of the most varied nature so long as they

> possess demonstrated functional significance for the individual. (Hall & Lindzey, 1957, p. 17)

Of all personality theorists, the thinking of Gordon Allport appears to have the most direct relevance to semiotic psychology. For Allport (1961) personality is "the dynamic organization within the individual of those psychophysical systems that determine his/her characteristic behavior and thought." Allport defines each of the terms in this definition as follows.

"Dynamic organization" means the forming of patterns of hierarchies of ideas and habits. "Psychophysical" means personality is neither exclusively mental nor exclusively physical; its organization entails the functioning of both "mind" and "body" in some inextricable unity. The term *system* means a complex of elements in mutual interaction. *Determine* means that personality is something and does something. The latent psychological systems, when called into action, either motivate or direct specific activity and thought. All the systems that comprise personality are to be regarded as *determining tendencies*. They exert a directive influence on all the formal and expressive acts by which the personality becomes known. *Characteristic* means that all behavior and thought are characteristic of the person and *unique* to him or her. We share some acts and concepts and some are more idiosyncratic than others, but none lacks a personal flavor. "Behavior" and "thought" cover anything whatsoever the individual may do. Behavior and thought are modes of adjustment elicited by the environment. The psychophysical systems that comprise personality select and direct these modes of adjustment (Allport, 1961).

The concept of motivation is fundamental to understanding personality, and it is the phenomenon of primary concern of psychologists who study personality. For some psychologists the study of motivation and needs is equal to the study of personality (Allport, 1961). By referring to Allport's definition, the central importance of motivation is apparent when we consider that it is necessary for something to cause or induce "behavior and thought." A motive is any internal condition of an individual that causes or induces behavior and thought.

Historically, there have been several problems associated with the use of the word *motivation*. First, a wide variety of terms have been invoked to describe motivation: *drive*, *urge*, *need*, and *desire* are examples. Second, some theorists have proposed a separate and unique motivation for a vast array of particular behaviors: mother love and pugnacity are examples (Klineberg). Finally, and most problematic, is that some theorists propose that the inducement for certain behaviors and thoughts is instinctive. The problem with the term 'instinct' is its association with the idea that the stimulus for behavior is genetically inherited. Many psychologists are concerned with motivations that are fundamental and widespread to the extent that they appear to be instinctive when in fact they are learned. These psychologists employ the term 'need' to avoid the implication that they are referring to inherited behavior. The concept of need avoids entirely the nature-nurture controversy. The implicit definition of a need is that it is learned. As with attitudes, this means that a need allows for conscious consideration and change.

2. Interpersonal Needs

On the armature of the motivational dimension of personality, William Schutz has constructed a theory of interpersonal behavior (Schutz, 1966). He drew especially on psychodynamic (i.e., Freudian) personality theory in developing his *postulate of interpersonal needs.* The postulate of interpersonal needs states that "(a) every individual has three interpersonal needs: inclusion, control and affection; and (b) inclusion, control and affection constitute a sufficient set of areas of interpersonal behavior for the prediction and explanation of interpersonal phenomena" (p. 13). The psychodynamic aspect of his theory is the position of the self-concept as the primary motivation for the satisfaction of interpersonal needs.

As the wording of the postulate of interpersonal needs indicates, Schutz was trained in the philosophy of science, and he gave careful consideration to presenting his theory in a scientific way. In practical terms, this means that at every step of the way Schutz was concerned with providing operational definitions for the elements of his theory, starting with the basic terms: interpersonal, interpersonal situation, need, and interpersonal need.

Schutz defines "interpersonal" as relationships that occur between people. It may be stating what is obviously contained in the word "interpersonal," but he is concerned with emphasizing that the psychological presence of another person (or persons) produces behavior that would not occur if this person (or persons) were not present. An interpersonal situation is one in which an individual takes account of another individual to make some decision. An interpersonal situation is one in which one of the criteria in a person's decision making process leading to a behavioral response is the expectation of the reaction of other persons present to that behavioral response.

Schutz defines a "need" as "a situation or condition of an individual the nonrealization of which leads to undesirable consequences." In other words, according to Schutz, a need is a psychological state that causes people to think and act in such a manner as to attain a specific goal. But, and this is a very important but, the "undesirable consequences" part of his definition means that the inability to attain the goal related to the psychological state creates mental problems. An interpersonal need "is one that may be satisfied only through the attainment of a satisfactory relation with other people." The inability of a person to satisfy an interpersonal need may lead to mental problems that range from mild anxiety, or in extreme cases, when the inability to attain any satisfactory interpersonal relationship is prolonged, to death wishes.

The interpersonal need for inclusion is the motivation to establish and maintain satisfactory relationships with people in terms of interaction and association. Some words that describe the dimension of the relationships related to the interpersonal need for inclusion are: associate-isolate; interact-withdraw; and, extravert-introvert. The positive expression of the interpersonal need for inclusion is the individual's desire to be with other people and to want other people include them in their activities. The negative expression would be the opposite: the individual's desire *not* to be with people and *not* to have people include them in their activities.

The interpersonal need for control is the motivation to establish and maintain satisfactory relationships with people in terms of power and influence. Some words that describe the dimension of the relationships related to the interpersonal need for control are: dominance versus submission; leader versus follower; and giving orders versus taking orders. The positive expression of the interpersonal need for control is the individual's desire to be in charge of things when they are with people and to want people to let them be in charge of things. The negative expression would be the opposite: the individual's desire *not* to be in charge of things when they are with people and *not* to want people to let them be in charge of things.

The interpersonal need for affection is the motivation to establish and maintain satisfactory relationships with people in terms of love and friendship. Some words that describe the dimension of the relationships related to the interpersonal need for affection are: like versus dislike; emotionally close versus emotionally distant; and, disclosing feelings versus hiding feelings. The positive expression of the interpersonal need for affection is the individual's desire to be fond and tender with another person and to want another person to be fond and tender with him or her. The negative expression would be the opposite: the individual's desire *not* to be fond and tender with another person and *not* to want another person to be fond and tender with him or her. The need for affection differs from the needs for inclusion and control in that affection is dyadic, that is, it only occurs between two people at any given time; in contrast, inclusion and control relations can occur either in dyads or in groups.

Schutz summarizes his definitions of the three interpersonal needs as follows:

> With respect to an interpersonal relationship, inclusion functions primarily during the formation of a relationship, whereas control and affection function primarily during existing relationships. Inclusion is always concerned with whether a relationship exists. Within existing relationships, control is the area concerned with who gives orders and makes decisions, whereas affection is concerned with how emotionally close or distant the relationship becomes. Thus, inclusion operates in terms of *in* or *out*, control in terms of *top* or *bottom*, and affection in terms of *close* or *far*. (p. 24)

3. Personality Traits

The previous chapter indicated that the favored concept in social psychology is attitude, which was defined as a relatively permanent predisposition to respond in a certain way to sign stimuli, e.g., language and paralanguage. There is a mental set called forth, but there is not a particular overt behavioral response that is necessary for a mental set to be labeled an attitude. Attitudes are a form of sign behavior and are linked to classical Pavlovian conditioning through the mediation process that is portrayed in Figures 1.8 and 2.4.

An attitude is a single-domain concept that attempts to explain only the mental set towards a specific stimulus. In the study of personality, where the concern is with the explanation of varied behaviors which are functionally equivalent for a particular individual, the favored concept is 'trait.' The concept of trait includes stimuli, mental sets and responses. The emphasis on stimuli and responses indicates what differentiates a trait from an attitude. A trait is a mental set in which many different stimuli are rendered functionally equivalent, and in addition, the mental set induces one of several different overt behavioral responses that are also functionally equivalent. Allport (1961) uses the example of a trait which he labels a 'communist phobia.' Following Allport's thinking, a person with a communist phobia has a mental set that causes several different stimuli to be perceived *as if* they were the same thing, in this case 'communistic.' Some stimuli perceived as being functionally equivalent to a person with a communist phobia are: Russians, sex education in the public schools, labor unions, and atheism. At the same time there are overt behavioral responses induced by the mental set 'communistic.' The person with a communist phobia will engage in one or more different behaviors that they consider appropriate and functionally equivalent: picketing the Russian embassy, writing letters of protest to the school board, throwing stones at strikers, call atheists un-American. Figure 3.1 portrays this complex of events in terms of the mediation process. This figure shows that ". . . a trait is determined by the equivalence of stimuli that arouse it and by the equivalence of responses that it provokes" (Allport, 1961, p. 322).

Figure 3.1

In his book *The Interpersonal Underworld*, Schutz (1966) summarized a vast literature on the theories associated with social motivation and research on interpersonal behavior, and from this summary he identified the functionally equivalent stimuli, the mental sets, and the functionally equivalent responses that are associated with each of the three interpersonal needs. He has employed this extensive knowledge to create a taxonomy of interpersonal traits. For an interpersonal trait the stimuli are persons and the responses are interpersonal behaviors. An interpersonal mental set has two dimensions, the attitude of the individual towards others ($s \rightarrow o$), and the individual's perception of others' attitude towards themselves ($o \rightarrow s$). Figure 3.2 indicates the situation of functionally equivalent stimuli: different persons; the interpersonal mental set: $s \rightarrow o$ = "I don't like

Figure 3.2

people," o→s = "People don't like me," and the functionally equivalent interpersonal responses. These are the elements of the interpersonal personality trait that Schutz labels "undersocial."

Schutz's use of Freudian theory comes to the fore in his use of self-concept as the motivating force behind the strength of an interpersonal need. The individual's self-concept (s->s) determines whether the strength of a need is too little, too much, or appropriate. Schutz calls these levels of strength of interpersonal needs "deficient," "excessive," and "ideal." For example, persons whose self-concept, or attitude towards themselves, is "I am insignificant," may be either deficient or excessive in their attempt to satisfy the interpersonal need for inclusion. Their interpersonal behavior is the determining factor in whether

INCLUSION

NEED STRENGTH →	Deficient	Excessive	Ideal
TRAIT LABEL →	Undersocial	Oversocial	Social
Mental Set			
self to other →	I'm not interested in people.	I'm not really interested in people.	I'm interested in people.
other to self →	People are not interested in me.	People are not really interested in me.	People are interested in me.
self to self →	I am insignificant.	I am insignificant.	I am significant.
Interpersonal Behavior	Non-association and interaction. Lack of involvement. Late to meetings. Inordinate number of conflicting. engagements. "I'm sorry I can't stay too long."	Constantly seeks out people and wants people to seek him/her out. Can't stand to be alone.	Comfortable with people or alone. Can be a high or a low participant in a group. Capable of either strong commitment or no commitment.

Figure 3.3

they are classified as undersocial or oversocial. The Freudian point is that the underlying motivation is the same for both the undersocial and oversocial individuals. Figures 3.3, 3.4 and 3.5 summarize Schutz's model of the interpersonal traits.

The first section of this chapter stated that personality theorists use the term *need* to avoid the nature-nurture controversy. Schutz makes this point very clear in his discussion of pathological behavior. For Schutz, psychoses, psychopathic behavior, and anxiety are the results of unsatisfactory interpersonal relations. These mental problems are the result of the inability of an individual to establish and maintain satisfying interpersonal relations in terms of inclusion, control, and affection. This is not to deny that physical problems may impede or preclude the satisfaction of one or more interpersonal needs. However, an interpersonal theory of personality asserts that barring any physical or biologically abnormal circumstance, pathological social behavior is learned, is the result of harsh interpersonal

CONTROL

NEED STRENGTH →	Deficient	Excessive	Ideal
TRAIT LABEL →	Abdicrat	Autocrat	Democrat
Mental Set			
self to other →	I don't really respect people.	I don't trust people.	I respect and trust people.
other to self →	People don't really respect me.	People don't trust me.	People respect and trust me.
self to self →	I am incompetent.	I am incompetent.	I am competent.
Interpersonal Behavior			
	Submissive. Gravitates to subordinate positions with no responsibility for decisions and someone else in charge. Follower. Loyal lieutenant.	Dominating. Power seeker. Always has to be the one in charge and the one to give orders. Wants to be responsible for everything.	Comfortable giving or not giving orders. Can be submissive, dominant, or neither, depending on the situation. Can be a leader or a follower.

Figure 3.4

AFFECTION

NEED STRENGTH →	Deficient	Excessive	Ideal
TRAIT LABEL →	Underpersonal	Overpersonal	Personal
Mental Set			
self to other →	I don't like people.	I don't really like people.	I like people.
other to self →	People don't like me.	People don't really like me.	People like me.
self to self →	I am unlovable.	I am unlovable.	I am lovable.
Interpersonal Behavior	Avoids close personal ties. Relationships are superficial and distant. Rejects/avoids emotional closeness. Subtle: appears friendly to everyone.	Direct: overt attempts to gain approval by being extremely personal, intimate, and confiding. Subtle: stops friends from having other friends.	Can be personal or distant. If not liked, can accept the fact that the dislike is the result of a relationship and not that they are "unlovable."

Figure 3.5

relations, and, therefore, when these harsh relations are changed, it is possible for the individual with the pathological manifestations to change.

B. Culture and Personality

1. Social Roles[1]

The study of social roles represents the principle meeting ground between anthropology and psychology in that a role is the connecting link between an individual's culture and an individual's personality. The anthropologist Ralph Linton provided the definitive statement of the concept *role* that points to the intertwining of culture and personality: "[R]ole will be used to designate the sum total of the cultural patterns associated with a particular status. It thus includes the attitudes, values and behaviors ascribed by the society to any and all persons occupying this status" (Linton, 1945, p. 46).

A status is the particular position that an individual occupies in a social system. Every status is associated with a social position: father, professor, physician, and employer. The culture provides the ready-made answers as to the relative importance of each of these social positions, and the correct behavior expected by each individual occupying each social position. Every social position is ranked in terms of importance and power, and the relative ranking of a social position is the indication of its status.

Every social interaction involves reciprocal role relationships, which, given the statuses of the individuals interacting, determine the range of the behaviors emitted. The implication of this statement is that the only way that personality becomes extensional is through role performance. There is no social behavior that is not the expression of some social role. In a society in which there are no buses there are no bus drivers, and vice versa, an individual cannot perform the behavior associated with being a bus driver in a society in which there are no buses. This statement does not mean that every bus driver behaves in exactly the same manner. In fact, the role 'bus driver,' like every role, has a range of permissible behaviors associated with it, and it is by choosing from this permissible range of behaviors that the personality of a particular bus driver is expressed. Figure 3.6 shows 'role expectation' and 'role performance' as cultural stimuli and cultural responses, respectively. The figure indicates how the personality of the individual mediates between the role expectation and the role performance through the individual's perception of and attitude towards the role. When the word *role* appears alone it refers to the entire complex of explicit and implicit behaviors indicated in Figure 3.6.

The position 'bus driver' is an explicit and identifiable role. There are, however, roles that are not quite so explicit, for example, age and sex roles. In fact, social status according to one's age and sex is a universal phenomenon in that every culture has rules as to the appropriate behavior associated with individuals of different ages and of each sex. In some societies older people are venerated for their years of experience; in other societies older people are perceived as having lost their

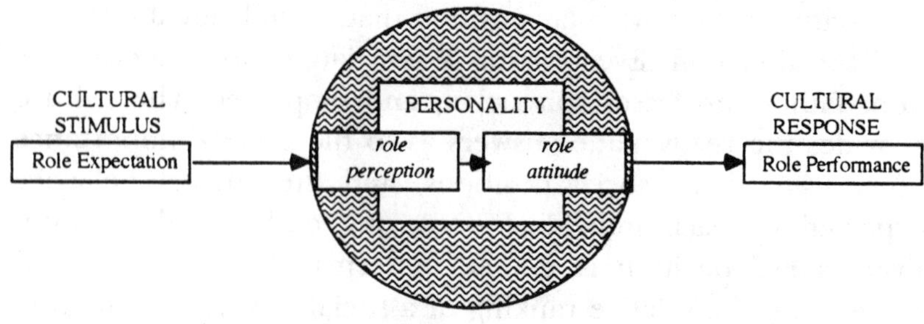

Figure 3.6

ability to contribute. In some societies the most 'macho' men may wear skirts, in others, a man wearing a skirt would be looked upon with scorn. In this manner the culture prescribes the role expectations and prescribes the appropriate role performance.

The emphasis on *cultural* stimuli and *cultural* responses should not be interpreted as being an indication that culture is a more important variable than the individual. On the contrary, as Figure 3.6 indicates, the role expectation and the role performance are mediated through the thinking and emotive states of specific individuals, and just as there can be no social behavior that is not associated with a particular role, there can be no social role unless there is some individual personality to perform this role. For this reason this section is labeled culture-and-personality, the dashes linking two concepts that, although they can be independently analyzed, have a real life existence that is interdependent.

2. Modes of Behavior

The anthropologist Edward Hall (1959), has proposed a theory in which it is hypothesized that culture is characterized by three modes of social behavior: the formal, the informal and the technical.

> Trager[2] and I arrived at this tripartite theory as a result of some . . . observations as to the way in which Americans talk about and handle time. We discovered that there were three kinds of time: formal time, which everyone knows about and takes for granted and is well worked into daily life; informal time, which has to do with situational or

> imprecise references like "a while," later," "in a minute;" [and] . . . technical time, an entirely different system used by scientists and technicians in which even the terminology may be unfamiliar to the non-specialist. . . . we discovered that [there are] three modes of behavior. (p. 64)

Hall has developed a taxonomy that classifies the modes of behavior based on the manner in which (1) the person learned the behavior, (2) the person's cognitive state in relation to the behavior, and (3) the person's attitude towards the behavior.

Hall identifies three ways in which a person has learned a particular behavior that are significant in identifying whether the mode of behavior is formal, informal, or technical. For the formal mode the learning is by admonition. The person has exhibited behavior in a particular situation and has been told "you *don't* do that!" Learning of the formal mode is by trial and error, which means that the person emits behavior that is then responded to by a significant other in a binary and dogmatic fashion: it is either correct or incorrect. The word "told" should be in quotation marks, because the injunction against the behavior can be applied nonverbally. A glance or a tone-of-voice can signal that some transgression has occurred and serve the same function as a spoken "you don't do that!" For the informal mode of behavior the learning is by imitation. Persons usually have a particular individual, or category of individuals, after whom they model their behavior. The informal mode is learned by copying behavior that is perceived as being appropriate, and the success of the individual is determined by the ability to reproduce the behavior in question. If an individual has asked how to perform a particular role and the answer is "it depends," that is the indication that the learning is of an informal nature. For the technical mode the learning is by explanation. The person has been taught by someone acting as a teacher who has explained to him or her what to do. The technical mode is learned by following instructions, and success depends on the ability to follow the teacher's explanation of what to do. Technical learning is a one-way street in which all knowledge rests with the teacher.

The second identifying characteristic of a mode of behavior is the person's cognitive state in relation to that behavior. In the formal mode individuals are completely unconscious of the behavior they are producing. Persons, if asked, cannot give a verbal account of their behavior in terms of how or why they are behaving in that particular manner. This is not to say that the person cannot ultimately become conscious of the behavior in some manner but to become conscious of behavior that has been learned by precept and admonition is not a simple matter. In the informal mode the cognitive state is 'out-of-awareness,' which is to say persons when asked to give a verbal account of their behavior, may not be able to do this immediately, but in a short time, if they think about it, can provide such a verbal description. In the technical mode of behavior individuals are completely conscious of what they are doing, and can with great ease describe the 'hows' and 'whys' of their behavior.

The third identifying characteristic of a mode of behavior is the attitude of the person towards the behavior. Such attitudes can vary from extremely strong, either for or against, to neutral. In the formal mode the attitude is extremely strong, the behavior is either completely accepted or completely rejected. Behavior that has been learned in a dogmatic manner and which is completely unconscious, that is the formal mode, is reacted to as if it were 'human nature.' In the informal mode the attitudes, either pro or con, will be mild. In the technical mode there are essentially no feelings involved, the individual is neutral in terms of liking or disliking. In the pristine form of the technical mode the issue of acceptance or rejection would not even come up.

3. Power and Solidarity

Every society has a myriad of specific social positions that involve particular tasks, and as was indicated, each such social position has a relative ranking, or status. We have also discussed the more superordinate classification of social positions based on age and sex, which also have differential social statuses. There are two other such superordinate relationships between persons-power and solidarity that may be expressed in overt behavior during role performance. In other words, the personality of the person will express itself in any given social interaction in terms of the performance prescribed for the

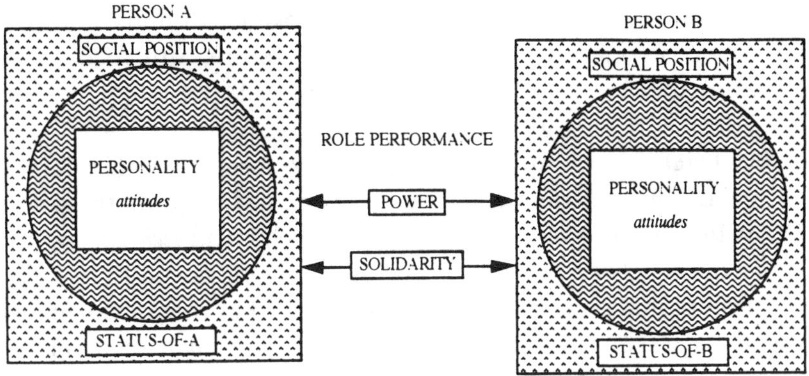

Figure 3.7

specific role (e.g., bus driver). In addition, there may be aspects of individuals' behavior that are associated with not only age and sex but also with the power and solidarity relationship they maintain with the person with whom they are interacting. Figure 3.7 presents a model of this situation.

Interpersonal power is the extent to which one person can control the behavior of another person. In their classic work "The Pronouns of Power and Solidarity," Brown and Gilman (1960) describe language phenomena that demonstrate the operation of the power and solidarity dimensions of interpersonal relationships. These authors trace the historical development of two singular pronouns of address in Europe that derived from the Latin words *tu* and *vos* (*tu* and *usted* in Spanish, *tous* and *vous* in French, etc.). Both words are translated as "you" in English; however, the first is for relationships that are relaxed and informal, whereas the second is for relationships that are courteous and formal. Following Brown and Gilman, I will use T to refer to the first, relaxed and informal, and V to the second, courteous and formal. It is noteworthy that these authors are pointing to the social control of behavior that is achieved by means of a "semantic" that references an interpersonal non-reciprocal power relationship. That is, a more powerful individual uses T with everyone, but everyone else must use V when speaking to her or him. An example of this behavior is that "in medieval Europe, generally, the nobility said T to the common people and received V; the master of a household said T to his slave, and his servant and his squire, and received V. Within the family, of whatever social level, parents gave T to children and were given V" (pp. 306-307).

In brief, Brown and Gilman have proposed that an interpersonal dimension can be abstracted from such asymmetrical relationships as *older than*, *parent of*, *employer of*, and *richer than*, and that the label for this dimension is "more powerful than." This interpersonal power dimension is reflected in role performance in that persons with greater power can perform in a relaxed and informal manner with those of lesser power, and persons with less power must perform in a courteous and formal manner with those of greater power.

Interpersonal solidarity is the extent to which two persons have similar attitudes. Neither a physical attribute such as eye color nor frequency of personal contact necessarily affect the solidarity between two persons. It is, rather, attitudes related to politics, religion, male-female relationships, and such, that are the factors that contribute to interpersonal solidarity. "Not every personal attribute counts in determining whether two people are solidary enough to use the mutual T [that is, to be relaxed and informal with each other]. . . . The similarities that matter seem to be those that make for like-mindedness or similar behavior dispositions" (p. 309).

In brief, Brown and Gilman proposed a second interpersonal dimension that can be abstracted from such symmetrical relationships as: *vote for the same politicians, attend the same church,* and *have the same view of women's liberation* and that this dimension can be labeled "like minded." This interpersonal solidarity dimension is reflected in role performance in that persons who are "like-minded" behave with each other in a relaxed and informal manner, whereas persons who are not "like-minded," behave with each other in a courteous and formal manner.

PART II

SPEECH SIGNS

4

Linguistic Signs

A. Phonetics

In listening to speech one hears a continuous stream of sounds separated into breath groups. Sounds in the stream are not separated from each other in any consistent manner. At this first level of analysis linguists provide themselves with a method of entering this continuum of behavior. If you say the word 'maiden' and become very conscious of the movement of your lips and tongue, you will demonstrate to yourself a continuum of speech sounds. You will notice that there is continuous movement from the time you start the 'm' until the tip of your tongue reaches the upper teeth. Trying to describe everything that was going on with your lips, your tongue, and in your throat while you were producing just this one word would take much time. But, if you will repeat the word slowly, you will notice that there are points of maximum closure and maximum openness of the lips and tongue. These crests and troughs are the centers of segments of sounds that have indefinite borders, and it is at these points that we enter the continuum of speech behavior. Schematically:

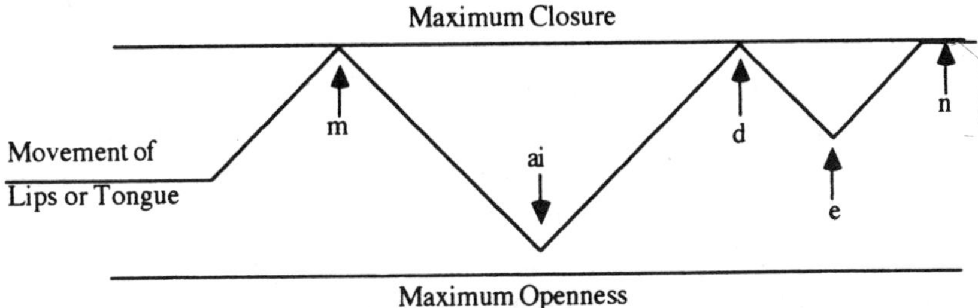

The arrows point to the centers of the segments.

The next task is to describe the sounds that occur at these centers. All the sounds are physical events that have three main aspects: (1) *Physiological*, the movement of the organs involved in producing the sound; (2) *Acoustic*, the nature of the sound waves set in motion by the speech apparatus; and (3) *Auditory*, the transformation of the sound wave by the ear and the central nervous system into the perception of speech. Linguists have found the *physiological* aspect the most convenient of the three for description of sounds. There are several reasons why the physiological aspect is convenient. First, it is possible to observe directly the movements and positions of the vocal organs. Second it is possible to imitate the movements and positions of the vocal organs without any special equipment. Third, it is possible to unambiguously and simply describe any language sound in terms of the movements that produce it. Fourth, after some practice it is easy to convert a physiological description of a sound into the sound itself by simply making the movement specified.

The physiological mechanisms that are involved in producing sounds are employed by linguists to establish a matrix, or *phonetic chart*, which defines the cardinal value of any sound. The parameters of this physiological matrix are:

(1) *The point of articulation*. This is the point of maximum constriction in the mouth or pharynx. For the 'd' in *maiden*, it occurs when the apex of the tongue reaches the alveolar ridge. *Apex* and *alveolar ridge* are technical phonetic terms referring to the tip of the tongue and the bumpy ridge immediately behind the teeth, respectively.

(2) *The degree of air-stream interruption*. If the air-stream is blocked completely during the articulation the sound is a *stop*. If the air-stream is only partially blocked producing friction, the sound is a *fricative*. If the constriction is not narrow enough to produce any degree of friction, and the only function of the mouth and nose is to modify a sound produced by the vocal cords, that sound is called *resonant*.

(3) *The vocal cords*. If the vocal cords are active at the time of articulation, the sound is *voiced*. If the cords are not vibrating at the time of articulation, the sound is *voiceless*. If you

put your hand on your throat and say the word 'din,' first normally and then in a whisper, you will feel the vocal cords vibrating during the normal pronunciation but not for the whisper.

Having chosen a method for segmenting the sound continuum and providing for the classification of the segments, the linguist now has a frame of reference from which the vocal production of any speaker can be described. Furthermore, this method for providing *phonetic units* assures her or him and any other interested observer that different linguists working on the same continuum of speech sounds will arrive at the same conclusions regarding the phonetic units in that continuum.

B. Phonemics

1. Segmental Phonemes

The segmentation of the continuum of speech sounds provides the linguistic raw data. The linguist next performs a series of operations on these raw data that will reduce their complexity and permit them to be described parsimoniously. The first level of this analysis, the description of the sound system of a language, is called *phonemics*. The unit of description at this level of analysis is the *phoneme*, which is a class of speech sounds mutually exclusive of any other such class. The member sounds of each phoneme, the *allophones*, share some feature of articulation, or some combination of features, and show characteristic patterns of distribution.

A phonemic analysis can be demonstrated by examining the initial sounds in <cut> and <coat>. Arrowheads, < >, are used when referring to words written in the usual letters of the alphabet. On saying these words, a native speaker of English will find that the point of articulation of the initial sounds is different and distinct. For the <c> in <cut> the *back of the tongue* moves forward and upwards towards the roof of the mouth. For the <c> in <coat> the *back of the tongue* moves up and back into the throat. The two sounds produced are written in phonetic spelling as [k] and [q], respectively. The feature of articulation shared by both of these phonetic units is the movement of the *back of the tongue*. The square brackets [ ] are used when referring to phonetic spelling.

If all occurrences of the [k] and [q] sounds in English are examined, we would find that [k] occurs only preceding vowels made with the tongue advanced in the mouth, and [q] occurs only preceding vowels made with the tongue retracted (pulled back) in the mouth. These facts demonstrate the principle of *complementary distribution*: each of the phonetic units occurs in a specific context in which the other never occurs. On the basis of their phonetic similarity, that is the movement of the back of the tongue, and complementary distribution, [k] and [q] are analyzed as being members of one class of sounds that is called the phoneme 'k,' which is written /k/. The [k] and [q] are then *allophones* of /k/. The diagonal lines / / are used when referring to phonemic spelling.

There is another pattern of distribution of phonetic units that is created by repeated productions of one unit. If we were to measure everything that could possibly be measured about the [k] in repeated occurrences of <cut>, we would discover that they are not exactly alike. A plot of the differences of each would result in a normal curve with the unit we call [k] as the mean. This type of distribution is called *non-distinctive variation.* The non-distinctive variation of the [k] forms a subclass of sounds of the allophone [k]. Only acoustic instruments or a highly skilled phonetician can detect non-distinctive variation.

To establish each phoneme of a language as different and distinct from every other phoneme, the principle of *contrast* is invoked. To show contrast, varying phonetic units are substituted at one point in a word while all the other units are held constant. If another word is produced that is distinct in sound and means something else to a native speaker, contrast has been shown, and the existence of a distinct phoneme is established. For example, as we have just seen, in English there is the phoneme /k/ consisting of [k] ~ [q]. The ~ is short hand for "in complementary distribution with." Similarly, there is a phoneme /g/ consisting of [g] ~ [G]. If in the word <till> a [k] or a [g] is substituted for the <t>, or if in the word <tore> a [q] or a [G] is substituted of the <t>, four new words are produced: <kill>, <gill>, <core> and <gore>. To a native speaker of English each of these four words is distinct in the way it sounds and in what it means. This type of contrast justifies the existence of a /k/ phoneme and a /g/ phoneme in English. The /k/ has the allophones [k] ~ [q], and the /g/ has the allophones [g] ~ [G].

In the preceding discussion we have been careful to use the qualification "native speaker of English." This distinction emphasizes the fact that there is no general /k/ or /g/ for every language. The linguistically unsophisticated native speaker of English is rather hard put to find a difference between the initial sounds of <cut> and <coat>, but to a linguistically unsophisticated speaker of Arabic this difference would be immediately apparent. The English speaker has a /k/ with [k] ~ [q], but for the Arabic speaker [q] is part of a different phoneme. The point here is that the /k/ of English and the /k/ of Arabic are not identical.

2. Suprasegmental Phonemes

The phonetic units of the language that proceed in one-dimensional time succession are called *segmental phones*. The analysis of these phonetic units yields the *segmental phonemes*. These are what the layman recognizes as the vowels and consonants of the language. In addition, there are also prosodic features of *length, loudness, tone*, and *manner of termination* that occur simultaneously with the segmental phones. The descriptive linguist records the discriminable variations of these prosodic features and subjects them to the same type of analysis as is used for segmental phones. The contrasting classes that result from this analysis are called the *prosodic* or *suprasegmental phonemes* of the language.

If the word <pin> is said a number of times to the speaker of English, each time increasing the amount of time spent on the <i>, a word is never produced which she or he will say is different in meaning from any of the other words. In fact, it is not possible to find any word in English in which, by increasing the length of one of the segmental units, another word can be produced which has a different meaning. Since contrast does not exist, this feature of length is not phonemic in English. This phenomenon is not true of all languages. In Finnish <peli> means "damper," but increasing the length of the <l> produces another word meaning "game." This example offers evidence for establishing length as being phonemic in Finnish. In such a manner the suprasegmental phonemes of each language are identified.

Loudness. The loudness of a phonetic unit (i.e., a phone) depends primarily on the force with which air is expelled from the lungs and secondarily on the energy with which the articulation is performed. The degree of loudness is approximately the same for all English monosyllabic words said in isolation. This degree of loudness is called *strong* and is used as a standard of measurement for other degrees of loudness. If you say <permit> once stressing the <e> and once stressing the <i>, you will produce two words different in sound and meaning. This difference in sound and meaning shows that stress is phonemic in English. The degree of loudness on the stressed versions of the <e> and <i> is relatively close to that degree of loudness used with monosyllables in isolation. The degree of loudness on the unstressed <e> and <i> is much less than that of their stressed versions, or of any monosyllable said in isolation. The degree of loudness on the stressed <e> and <i>, and on monosyllables said in isolation, are conditioned variations of the standard strong loudness, and are allophones of the phoneme *primary stress.* The weak loudness of the unstressed <e> and <i> are allophones comprising a *weak stress* phoneme.

Tone. The tone of our speech sounds is a function of the tension of the vocal cords and of their consequent rate of vibration. As with loudness, to demonstrate that pitch is phonemic in English, multisyllabic words or longer sentences are used, since it is *relative pitch* that is contrasted. The standard is the normal pitch of a speaker. This normal pitch varies from speaker to speaker and for the same speaker when she or he is speaking loudly or softly. However, every speaker has a recognizable normal pitch of voice. Examine the sentence <He's going home>, said as a statement of fact, emphasizing *where* he's going and not the fact that he's going. Using lines to represent the pitch of the voice, the sentence is said like this:

(1) he's going home

The line immediately below <he's going> represents the normal pitch of the voice. The line above the <ho> represents a pitch about two or three notes above the normal. The line under the <me> represents a pitch about two or three times below the normal. Humming the words of this sentence will demonstrate this clearly. The examination of many English sentences reveals that these three levels of pitch are phonemic. They are in contrast with each other because substituting one for another creates a difference in meaning. For example, say the same sentence, again as a statement of fact, but this time emphasizing the fact that he's *going now* and not where he's going. Using lines to represent relative pitch, the sentence is now said like this:

(2) he's going home

The lines depict the shift in the higher pitch from "home" to "going," and a native speaker of English will attest to a concomitant shift in meaning.

The normal tone is referred to as 'mid,' the higher tone as 'high,' and the lower one as 'low.' These are written phonemically as /^{2}/, /^{3}/ and /^{1}/, respectively. In our sample sentences the pitch phonemes would be written as follows:

(1) ^{2}he's going ^{3}home^1

(2) ^{2}he's ^{3}going home^1

Tempo. The means by which sequences of phones are put together are called *junctural phenomena.* The word <nitrate> is an example of a sequence of segmental units with close transition between the members of the sequence. By changing the transition between the <t> and the <r> from close to more distant, another utterance is produced: <night-rate>, which has a different sound and a different meaning. A comparison of such utterances as <I scream> versus <ice cream>, <a name> versus <an aim>, shows that the difference between a close transition and a more open one is phonemic in English. All the allophones of the open transition are classed into the phoneme called *plus juncture* and symbolized as /+/.

There is another group of junctural phenomena that occur at places where /+/ would normally occur. A speaker uses these junctural phenomena to indicate that he or she is terminating a sentence or sequence of sentences. Say the following three sentences in the manner indicated by the conventional punctuation marks:

(1) He's going home.

(2) He's going home?

(3) He's going home but will be back soon.

These sentences demonstrate three distinct ways of terminating <home>. In (1) there is a rapid fading away of the voice into silence. In (2) there is a rapid but short rise in pitch and the voice appears to be sharply cut off. In (3) there is sustained pitch and a slight decrease in volume. This contrast shows that there are three *terminal juncture* phonemes in English: fading, or double cross, symbolized by +, rising, or double bar, symbolized by | |, and sustained, or single bar, symbolized by | .

3. A Sketch of English Phonemes

Consonant Phonemes. The consonant phonemes in English are as follows:

/p/	as in the words	<poor, pin, prove, pip>
/t/	as in the words	<take, tin, tree, tit>
/k/	as in the words	<key, cup, cough, kick>
/b/	as in the words	<boor, bin, bread, bib>
/d/	as in the words	<dim, din, dread, did>
/g/	as in the words	<give, grim, goose, gig>
/f/	as in the words	<fine, fin, frame, deaf>
/v/	as in the words	<vine, vim, vale, love>
/f/	as in the words	<fine, fin, frame, deaf>
/s/	as in the words	<sip, sin, soul, sis>
/z/	as in the words	<zip, zeal, zero, buzz>
/ʃ/	as in the words	<shall, smash, shake>
	(The ʃ is referred to as "esh.")	
/ʒ/	as in the words	<rouge, treasure, garage>
	(The ʒ is referred to as "ezh.")	
/ʧ/	as in the words	<watch, church>
	(The ʧ is referred to as "etch.")	
/ʤ/	as in the words	<jury, gin, Jack, judge>

(The ʤ is referred to as "edge.")
/θ/ as in the words <theater, thick, thin, both>
(The θ is referred to as "theta")
/ð/ as in the words <the, this, then, bathe>
(The ð is referred to as "edthe.")
/m/ as in the words <man, move, mill, mum>
/n/ as in the words <new, nudge, near, none>
/ŋ/ as in the words <sing, bang, ring>
(The ŋ is referred to as "engma.")
/l/ as in the words <light, let, laugh, lull>
/r/ as in the words <right, reek, roll>
/y/ as in the words <you, year, yeast>
/w/ as in the words <win, will, witch>
/h/ as in the words <hit, him, who>

Vowel Phonemes. The vowel phonemes in English, which are pronounced in the words indicated in all dialects of American English, are as follows:

/i/ as in the words <bit, miss, hill>
/e/ as in the words <bet, mess, bread>
/æ/ as in the words <bat, mass, plaid>
(The æ is referred to as "digraph.")
/ə/ as in the words <duck, but, flood>
(The ə is referred to as "shwa.")
/u/ as in the words <foot, full, put>

The following vowel phonemes in English are pronounced in the words indicated, but in some dialect areas these diagnostic words are pronounced with a different vowel. However, if the vowel indicated does occur in a particular dialect, it will occur in these words. It is important to note that in these examples the vowel has to be a single vowel and not a diphthong, because a dialect may not have the vowel as a single vowel but will have it as part of a diphthong.

/ɨ/ as in the word <children>
(The ɨ is referred to as "barred i.")
/a/ as in the words <not, pot, hot>
(However, this is /ɔ/ in Eastern New England.)
/o/ as in the words <home, whole>
/ɔ/ as in the words <cough, bought, wash>
(The ɔ is referred to as "open o.")

Diphthongs. The consonant phonemes /y/, /w/, /h/ and /r/ also occur following single vowels. When these four consonant phonemes operate in this manner, the resulting vowel-plus-consonant sequence is a *diphthong*. All the thirty-six possible diphthongs that result from the combination of the nine vowels in combination with these four consonants do occur. However, some of these diphthongs are extremely rare. It is beyond the scope of this book to discuss the dialect variations of these diphthongs. However, focusing on just a few words for which the pronunciation is stable across different dialect areas provides an idea of the nature of diphthongs; and the pronunciation of the four consonant phonemes /y/, /w/, /h/ and /r/ when they occur following a vowel.

/ey/ as in the words <bay, bale, bait>
/uw/ as in the words <do, boot>
(However, this is /ɨw/ in the South.)
/æh/ as in the words <yeah, baa>
("Baa" refers to the sound sheep make.)
/ir/ as in the word <dear>
(However, this is /ih/ in Eastern New England, the Mid-Atlantic and Southern states.)

4. Phonemes and Spelling

The reader will by now have become aware of the fact that regular spelling and phonemic spelling are not always the same. A frequent oversight on the part of both students and scholars studying language behavior is the fact that the sound system (i.e., the phonemes) of a language is not necessarily isomorphic to the writing system (orthography) of that language. In English there are two major aspects to the discrepancy between sounds and letters of the alphabet. The first is that one phoneme may be pronounced in response to several different letters or combinations of letters. For example, the phoneme /k/, that is, the sound that is pronounced, is the response to the letters of the alphabet <c> and <k>, as in <car> and <kill>. The most serious discrepancy of this type between sound and spelling in English is for the sound /ə/, which is pronounced in response to fifteen different letters or combination of letters of the alphabet: (1) <son>, (2) <does>, (3) <flood>, (4) <couple>, (5) <cup>, (6) <alone>, (7) <mountain>, (8) <system>, (9) <dungeon>, (10) <easily>, (11) <parliament>, (12) <gallop>, (13) <porpoise>, (14) <curious>, (15) <circus>.

The second type of discrepancy is that one letter of the alphabet is represented by several different phonemes. For example, four different phonemes, /s/, /ʃ/, /z/ and /ʒ/, are pronounced to the letter of the alphabet <s>: see, sugar, has, and measure. The most serious discrepancy of this type between sound and spelling in English is for the letter of the alphabet <o>, for which eight different vowels or diphthongs are pronounced:

(1) /i/	as in the word	<women>
(2) /a/	as in the word	<box>
(3) /o/	as in the word	<note>
(4) /ɔ/	as in the word	<order>
(5) /uw/	as in the word	<move>
(6) /u/	as in the word	<wolf>
(7) /ə/	as in the word	<son>
(8) /w/	as in the word	<choir>

C. Morphemics

The phonemic description of a language provides the data from which the linguist analyzes the various forms in which the phonemes occur. The unit of description at this level of analysis is the morpheme, which is a class of one or more minimum sequences of phonemes that has a unique function in the content structure of the language.

The identification of morphemes proceeds in a manner similar to that used for the identification of phonemes. Words are compared and differences in phonemic form are matched with differences in meaning. Partial similarity both in phonemic form and meaning requires a *morphemic cut* in one or both of the forms compared. The following words demonstrate this procedure: <boy>, <boys>, <boyish>; <girl>, <girls>, <girlish>; and, <bear>, <bears>, <bearish>. The sequence of phonemes used in <boy>, <girl> and <bear> occur many times in the language. Furthermore, each has a unique meaning attached to it that differs from the other two, or for that matter, from any other minimum sequence of phonemes in English. The fragments of the words left over from this classification, <-s> and <-ish> are also morphemes. They occur many times in the language and a native speaker will attest to their having unique meaning. We have, by this procedure, discovered five morphemes: <boy>, <girl>, <bear>, <-s> and <-ish>.

It is possible for a long morpheme to contain within it a sequence of phonemes comprising another morpheme. If removing the contained sequence destroys or drastically alters the unique meaning of the longer morpheme and leaves a residue that cannot be accounted for (that is, a residue to which no meaning can be attached), then the longer sequence retains its status as a morpheme. For example, the phoneme sequence /bɔy/ occurs in the words <boy> (/bɔy/) and <boil> (/bɔyl/), and the phoneme sequence /er/ occurs in the words <bear> (/ber/) and <air> (/er/), but all four words, <boy>, <boil>, <bear> and <air> are single morphemes because removing /bɔy/ from /bɔyl/ and /er/ from /ber/ leaves the residues /-l/ and /b-/, respectively, to which no meaning can be attached.

If two or more different minimum sequences of phonemes have the same meaning but can be shown to be in complementary distribution (C.D.) they are *allomorphs* of one morpheme. Consider, for example, the four words <hats>, <boys>, <glasses> and <oxen> which in phonemic transcription would be /hæts/, /bɔyz/, /glæsɨz/ and /aksɨn/.[1] Note that the <s> in <hats> is pronounced differently from the <s> in <boys>; and that the <es> in <glasses> is pronounced /ɨz/ and that the <en> in <oxen> is pronounced /ɨn/. Any native speaker of English would readily vouch for the fact that the /s/, /z/, /ɨz/ and /ɨn/ have the same meaning, that is, "more than one." Furthermore, an analysis of the occurrence of the /s/, /z/, /ɨz/ and /ɨn/ indicates that they are in complementary distribution. That is, the /s/, /z/ and /ɨz/ occur only after words that end in /t/, /y/ or /s/ and the /ɨn/ occurs only after the word <ox>.[2] Since /s/, /z/, /ɨz/ and /ɨn/ all share the same meaning and are in C.D., they are allomorphs of one morpheme: $\{-Z_1\}$. The dash (-) indicates that this morpheme is a suffix and can occur only by following and being attached to another morpheme. The subscript ($_1$) is a device to differentiate this particular morpheme from two other English morphemes that have similar pronunciation features but different meanings.

D. Syntactics

1. Orientation

Syntax examines the sequences of morphemes that are used to form the larger significant units of the language, and the classes of morphemes, or sequences of morphemes, that are identical in their grammatical function. The concept of the *constituent* is important at this stage of analysis. A constituent is any morpheme, or sequence of morphemes, that can be replaced by some other morpheme or sequence of morphemes. For example, the constituents of the word <boys> are <boy> and <-s>; this constituent analysis is a function of the fact that <girl> can be substituted for <boy> and <-ish> can be substituted for <-s>, and the resulting <girls> and <boyish> are both structurally meaningful sequences of morphemes. This constituent analysis shows that <boy> and <girl> are *identical in grammatical function*: nouns; and <-s> and <-ish> are identical in their grammatical function: noun suffixes. Notice that dictionary meaning has not entered at all into this constituent analysis. That fact that <boy> refers to "young male" and <girl> to "young female" is completely irrelevant to a constituent analysis. Even a nonsense word that fulfills a particular grammatical function can have grammatical meaning when it carries no referential meaning, for example <tove> as in "I saw some toves."

In an analogous manner the constituents of longer sequences of language are analyzed into their own constituents. In the case of longer sequences constituents are established in terms of the ability to substitute one word for any sequence of two or more words and maintaining *identical grammatical function.* For example, a first level of constituents of the sequence of words <the boys are from our school> is <the boys> and <are from our school> because <they> can be substituted for <the boys>: <they are from our school>; and <run> can be substituted for <are from our school>: <the boys run>. The identification of the constituents of <are from our school> as <are> and <from our school> is facilitated by the fact that a single word <good> can be substituted for the entire sequence <from our school> while maintaining *identical grammatical function*: <are good>.

The concept *identical grammatical function* is emphasized in the preceding paragraphs to call the attention of the reader to this important concept in a syntactic constituent class analysis. A vivid, and now classic, method of demonstrating this concept is by examining the following short excerpt from Lewis Carroll's poem *Jabberwocky*:

Twas brillig, and the slithy toves
Did gyre and gimble in the wabe;
All mimsy were the borogroves,
And the mome raths outgrabe.

Reading these four lines produces in any native speaker of English some sense of meaning; yet there is not one content word in these four lines that can be found in a dictionary. The meaning that is stimulated in the native speaker of English upon reading these four lines is the result of the fact that the nonsense words appear in very well established structural positions. These well established structural positions can be indicated by substituting blank spaces for the nonsense words:

Twas ________, and the ________y ________s
Did ________ and ________ in the ________;
All ________y were the ________s,
And the ________ ________s ________.

The blank spaces represent specific structural positions. English uses certain *words* exclusively in these structural positions, and this group of words performs an *identical grammatical function.* Even nonsense inserted in these structural positions stimulates a meaning–not dictionary meaning–grammatical meaning.

A *part of speech* is any group of constituents that are identical in their grammatical function. In analytical terms a particular part of speech is a class consisting of all words or sequences of words that can be substituted for a single word in a sentence. For example, for <the boys are from our school> words like <sweaters>, <best> and <swimmers> and sequences of words like <outstanding cheerleaders>, <most eloquent debate teams> and even nonsense words like <slithy toves> can all be substituted for the one word <boys>:

<the sweaters are from our school>
<the best are from our school>
<the swimmers are from our school>
<the outstanding cheerleaders are from our school>
<the most eloquent debate teams are from our school>
<the slithy toves are from our school>.

The fact that <sweaters>, <best>, <swimmers>, <outstanding cheerleaders>, <most eloquent debate teams>, and even <slithy toves>, can substitute for the single word <boy> indicates that these words and phrases belong to the same constituent class and represent therefore the same syntactic part of speech.

It is noteworthy that linguistic analysis in the preceding paragraph is a description of what people actually say, not a prescription of what they ought to say. The analysis of the syntactic parts of speech in English described in the next section is based on the work of Fries (1952). In the introduction to his book Fries states:

> The point of view in this discussion is descriptive, not normative or legislative. The reader will find here, *not* how certain teachers or textbook writers or "authorities" think native speakers of English ought to use the language, but how certain native speakers actually do use it in natural, practical conversations carrying on the various activities of a community. (p. 3)

To this end, Fries based his syntactic analysis of English on the recordings of fifty hours of actual conversations by 300 different speakers (viii).

2. A Sketch of English Syntax

Fries proposed, based on the constituent structure analysis of the recorded conversations, 19 parts of speech for spoken English. However, words classified as being members of four of these 19 parts of speech, specifically, nominals, verbals, adjectivals, and adverbials, account for 67 percent of all the words used in his sample. Furthermore, if each word in Fries's sample was counted only once, that is, when he did not count repetitions of the same word, words that were used as nominals, verbals, adjectivals, and adverbials accounted for 93 percent of the sample.

Nominals. The first structural position suggested by Fries, which he labeled the *Class 1* position, is demonstrated in the following sequences:

__________ is good.
__________ was good.
The __________ is good.
The __________ was good.
__________ s are good.
__________ s were good.
The __________ remembered the ______ .
The __________ went there.

Fries classifies any word that occurs in the blank in any of these or structurally similar diagnostic frames as a Class 1 word; or in other terminological schemes, a *nominal.*

The majority of words that can be used in the Class 1 position in these frames are 'nouns' in traditional grammar. The usual definition of a noun is 'the name of a person, place, or thing.' In the cases of the words 'John,' 'Detroit' and 'table,' if they are used in the sequences, 'John was bad,' 'Detroit is big,' and 'the tables are round,' the need for a new part of speech label, 'nominal,' to substitute for the label 'noun' appears to be superfluous. However, there are many words that can be used in one of the Class 1 positions which are not the names of persons, places or things. For example, 'possibility,' 'trouble,' 'electricity' and 'toves,' as in 'the possibility was great,' 'trouble is awful,' 'electricity is cheap,' and 'the toves went there.' The words 'possibility,' 'trouble,' 'electricity,' and the nonsense word 'toves,' are not the names of persons, places or things but because they occur in the Class 1 position in the diagnostic frames they are classified as nominals.

Verbals. The second structural position suggested by Fries, which he labeled the *Class 2* position, is demonstrated in the following diagnostic frames:

Sugar __________ good.
The book __________ good.
The books __________ good.
The clerk __________ the tax.
The clerks __________ the tax.
The team __________ there.
The teams __________ there.

Any word that is used in the blank in any of these diagnostic frames Fries classifies as a Class 2 word, or *verbal*. The majority of words that can be used in the Class 2 position in these frames are "verbs" in traditional grammar.

Adjectivals. The third structural position suggested by Fries, which he labeled the *Class 3* position, is demonstrated in the following diagnostic frames:

Sugar is ________.
The book is ________.
The books are ________.

Any word that is used in the blank in any of these diagnostic frames, is classified by Fries as a Class 3 word, or *adjectival*. The majority of words that can be used in the Class 3 position in these frames are known in traditional grammars as "adjectives."

Adverbials. The fourth structural position suggested by Fries, which he labeled the *Class 4* position, is demonstrated in the following diagnostic frames:

Adjectival Nominal is *Adjectival* ________.
(Example: Good company is valuable ________.)
The *Adjectival Nominal* is *Adjectival* ________.
(Example: The old man is necessary ________.)
Nominal remembered the *nominal* ________.
(Example: John remembered the book ________.)
The *Nominal* remembered the *nominal* ________.
(Example: The clerk remembered the reports ________.)
Nominal verbal ________.
(Example: John went ________.)
The *Nominal verbal* ________.
(Example: The group went ________.)

Any word that is used in the blank in any of these diagnostic frames, is classified by Fries as a *Class 4* word, or *adjectival*. Most words that can be used in the Class 4 position in these frames are known in traditional grammars as "adverbials."

Function Words. The four classes of words, nominals, verbals, adjectivals, and adverbials, account for the majority of words used by speakers of English. Fries reports that in a sample of conversational utterances nominals accounted for 39% of the words, verbals 25%, adjectivals 17% and adverbials 12%, that is, these four parts of speech account for 93% of the words spoken. The remaining 7% of the words in Fries's sample, those that were not used in any one of the four structural positions identified as nominal, verbal, adjectival, or adverbial, he labels *Function Words*. Fries reports that, although Function Words are frequent, only 154 different words account for all the occurrences of this syntactic category. This observation contrasts dramatically with the four major syntactic classes that contain thousands of separate items.

Fries identified fifteen structural positions that mark the Function Words, and are labeled *Class A* through *Class O*. Following is a brief sampling of several of these classes and a listing of some words that comprise these classes.

Class A: the, no, your, their, both, that, . . .
Class B: may, might, can, will, must, . . .
Class D: very, quite, really, pretty, too, . . .
Class E: and, both, either, not, but, . . .
Class F: at, by, from, up, across, . . .
Class I: when, where, how, who, which, . . .
Class J: after, when, because, so, since, . . .

Fries groups all fifteen diagnostic frames into the *Function Word* category. His justification for such a grouping is that for Function Words it is difficult, if not impossible, to separate their lexical meaning from their structural meaning. Take the sentence: the horse ran rapidly. It is not difficult to define what 'horse,' 'ran,' or 'rapidly,' means in the dictionary sense. That is to say that these three words describe actual experiences and have a referential meaning apart from any structural meaning which is indicated by their grammatical function. However, try to define 'the.' With some minor exceptions, words that do not occur in one of the four major syntactic positions are similar to the 'the' in that any meaning that they do carry is based solely on their grammatical function.

E. Semantics

1. Semantic Analysis

Semantics is the linguistic analysis of meaning. It is a field of study covering such topics as sound symbolism, thematic relations, the truth of sentences, plus a wide range of similar topics. Fromkin and Rodman (1988) describe the field of semantics as follows:

> For thousands of years philosophers have been pondering the meaning of 'meaning'; yet speakers of a language can understand what is said to them and can produce strings of words that convey meaning. Learning a language includes learning the 'agreed-upon' meanings of certain strings of sounds and learning how to combine these meaningful units into larger units that also convey meaning. We are not free to change the meanings of these words at will, for if we did we would be unable to communicate with anyone. . . . All speakers know how to combine words to produce phrase and sentence meaning. The study of the linguistic meaning of words, phrases and sentences is called semantics. (p. 162)

The content analysis described below is a taxonomy of meaning, one type of semantic analysis. It is a type of semantic analysis that is relevant to semiotic psychology because it is specifically designed to categorize speech signs in a manner such that the different content categories indicate different emotions and attitudes.

Louis A. Gottschalk has been for over thirty years concerned with systematically and objectively identifying the emotions and attitudes indicated by speech signs. The fact that he is by training a psychoanalyst has lent a particular thrust to his work, that is, the goal of understanding how a speaker's selection of particular words expresses the unconscious thoughts of that speaker. This aspect of the philosophic foundations of Gottschalk's work is stated by Levine in the Foreword to *The Measurement of Psychological States Through the Content Analysis of Verbal Behavior* (Gottschalk & Gleser, 1969):

> This book is a superb example of the application of diverse techniques to the understanding of human functioning and psycho-dynamics. The psychological techniques of skilled perception and empathic understanding of trends and hidden meanings, of seeing significant configurations and sequences, of understanding the intrapsychic and interpersonal forces at work, are used to develop categories of thematic content for the study of verbal productions. (p. v)

The important scientific aspect of Gottschalk's work is the fact that the reliability and validity of each of his scales for measuring emotions as they are expressed in verbal behavior has been tested in a large number of controlled research studies (Gottschalk & Gleser, 1969, chaps. III & V). Furthermore, there has accumulated over the years a large body of experimental evidence that demonstrates the efficacy of these scales (Gottschalk, 1979; Gottschalk, Lolas, & Viney, 1986).

2. Coding "Anxiety"

One prototype of the various content analysis scales developed by Gottschalk and his colleagues is the Anxiety Scale. The content categories of the Anxiety Scale were developed by Gottschalk on the basis of

> listening to many people who were considered to be anxious and not anxious and noting that there were categories of anxiety that were both relatively frequently present and readily identifiable. Further crystallization of the ideas for the descriptive features of the content items under each category heading came from listening to tape recordings of hypnotically induced anxiety states. (Gottschalk & Gleser, 1969, pp. 22–23)

Following is a brief and edited version of the Anxiety scale, with examples, based on the manual for using these scales developed by Gottschalk, Winget, and Gleser (1969).

* * *

a. References to Death: "I thought I was a goner."
b. References to Mutilation: "I broke my leg doing it."
c. References to Desertion and Abandonment: "I was there all by myself."
d. References to Ostracism: "He refused to be friends with me."
e. References to Loss of Support: "There was so much unemployment then."
f. References to Falling: "The baby mouse fell off the table."
g. References to Loss of Love: "My parents are separated."
h. References to Loneliness: "I live in a solitary kind of way."
i. References to Adverse Criticism: "She couldn't stand him."
j. References to Abuse: "I'm insulted by all this."

k. References to Condemnation: “I was cited for running a red light.”
l. References to Moral Disapproval: “Inside he knew he should have given them a better price for their car.”
m. References to Ridicule: “I'm being silly.”
n. References to Inadequacy: “I don't ever have anything interesting to “talk about.”
o. References to Shame and Embarrassment: “It's embarrassing for me to go into a room of strangers.”
p. References to Humiliation: “It's degrading to have to do things like that.”
q. Nonspecific References: “My father was in a real state.”

* * *

Following are two narratives that are reported in the Manual that have been coded for Anxiety (pp. 54-56). The transcript has been edited and the codes are the ones reported in the manual.

Sample #1

What do you want me to say? I don't[n] know what to talk about. Well, let's see, I don't[n] know what to talk about, Doc. I've been here for about four months, and had a pretty rough time of it. And and my wife, she wants me to stay here as long as I can. I told her I would. Our babies, they get on my nerves,[q] my little babies. Sometimes I don't get no sleep. I have a little cat at home. It got hurt,[b] it got a broken[b] leg and I had to get that fixed. I had a pretty rough time of it. My dad, I lost[a] my dad in ‘54, now only got two brothers living, and they never[c] come to see me. I guess it's pretty much my fault.[l] And my wife she changes her mind all the time. I think she's kind of nervous[q] too. She thinks she hears people saying bad[l] things about her. I get sort of frightened[q] and scared about it all. I don't know what else I can tell you. That's all I can think of.

Sample #2

n
Well, here I am again doing this. If I knew something to talk about, I could
tell it better. I don't know whether this goes over to the Board of Directors
n
or what, but I do the best I know how for a poor uneducated old man.
h
Everything I know about myself I like to keep to myself. Well, maybe the law
k k
is trying to find out about me. I was never arrested before in my life. I'd like
k k
to get arrested some times, just to see how it feels to go to jail. I guess I
n n n
sound like I'm off my rocker. But what little I know, why it ain't hardly worth
the telling. That nurse, she came to get more blood this afternoon. I just
b b
held out my arm she jabbed me with a needle. Seems like I'll run out of
b b
blood. I won't have any left. I've been jabbed so much now I got black and
l
blue spots on my arm. I don't know what'll happen to me after I make these
d
complaints. They might discharge me, even if I am sick.

The *Manual of Instructions for Using the Gottschalk-Gleser Content Analysis Scales* (Gottschalk et al., 1969) provides more detailed instructions for coding the Anxiety Scale and the procedures for preparing transcripts for coding. In addition, the manual provides instructions for coding two other types of content: Hostility and Social Alienation.

3. Content Analysis

It is appropriate to note at this point that the semantic content analysis developed by Gottschalk and his colleagues is just one of a wide variety of procedures labeled content analysis. The label 'content analysis' refers to research procedures ranging from counting inches of text in newspapers to identifying themes in folk songs (Holsti, 1968; Lomax & Halifax, 1968; Weber, 1990). The essential differences between various types of content analyses are not in terms of their general procedures but rather in terms of their focus and of the scope or inclusiveness of the material that is content analyzed. "[Content analysis] works through identifying and counting chosen units in a communication system . . . The units counted can be anything that the researcher wishes to investigate" (Fiske, 1990, p. 136). The content units counted by semiotic psychologists are speech units, that is, the linguistic and paralinguistic units of the speech channel.

In his *Signs, Language and Behavior,* Charles Morris (1946) provided a common terminology for all the disciplines concerned with sign-behavior. One result of Morris' efforts was his explication of three approaches to sign-behavior that he labels semantics, syntactics, and pragmatics. This categorization is a useful heuristic device for classifying the various content analyses that have been applied to speech signs.

According to Morris, semantics studies the relationship between signs and their referents. That is to say that the concern of semantics is the 'meaning' of signs. Syntactics studies the relationship of signs to each other, that is, the combination of signs without regard to their meaning or to the culture or personality of the users of the signs. Pragmatics studies the relationship between signs and the users of these signs; the ways in which signs relate to the culture and personality of the speakers and listeners.

Following this semiotic perspective, a content analysis of speech signs falls into one of three categories.

First, there is a semantic content analysis in which speech signs are classified in terms of their referents. A semantic content analysis categorizes words in a manner such that the different categories of words indicate different categories of reference. The content analysis developed by Gottschalk, described above, is an exemplar of one such categorization in that it categorizes words that refer to different affective states.

Second, there is a syntactic content analysis in which speech signs are classified in terms of how they are used in relationship to each other. A syntactic content analysis categorizes words in a manner such that different categories of words indicate different categories of relationships between words. The syntactic analysis developed by Fries, described above, is an exemplar of one such categorization in that it categorizes words in terms of their relationship to other words.

Third, there is a pragmatic content analysis, in which speech signs are classified in terms of their social or psychological function. A pragmatic analysis categorizes words in a manner such that the different categories of words indicate different categories of social or psychological function. An exemplar of this category of content analysis is presented in the chapter describing the work of Soskin and John.

5

Paralinguistic Signs

A. The Domain of Paralanguage

Speech signs consist of sounds that are either language or paralanguage. Language sounds are those that are essential for the production of the words in a language. For example, if I want to say the word "tin," it is essential that I produce a "t" sound, and this "t" sound is one that is used repeatedly to form words in English. However, if I cough it is equally apparent that the sound produced is not one that is used to produce words in English. All the sounds that are used to produce words in English would be language sounds for the speakers of English. All sounds not essential to word formation in English would be paralanguage sounds for the speakers of English.

The redundancy in referring to "speakers of English" is to emphasize the point that a particular sound may be a linguistic sound for the speakers of one language, while it may also be a paralinguistic sound for the speakers of another language (for example, the click sound of the Bantu languages).

Language is always accompanied by paralanguage. Whenever a speaker is producing sounds to form words, he or she is also producing sounds that are not essential to produce the words. For example, if I want to say the word "tin" I must say it with a certain level of loudness, which may range from a very soft whisper to a very loud shout. The particular loudness I choose to accompany the word "tin" is not, however, in any way essential to my forming it. Paralanguage also carries information. For example, a cough or shouting at a particular point in a conversation may so distract a person that he or she is completely unaware of the words used after the cough or accompanying the shout.

The language versus paralanguage distinction has an aspect that is of special interest for the study of semiotic psychology. An individual has very little option in either producing the specific sounds of language or in determining their distribution. To produce words the individual must produce highly standardized, specific sounds the quality of which cannot vary significantly when he or she intends to form words. If I want to say the word "tin," to produce the first sound my tongue must be placed so that the air coming out of my mouth is completely blocked. If my tongue is placed so that any air escapes when I want to say the "t" I will not say "tin" but "sin." On the other hand, an individual usually has a range of options in producing paralanguage. For example, I can produce a cough sound in a variety of ways: with my mouth open or completely closed; if open, the opening can vary from extremely narrow to extremely wide.

Similarly, the rules regulating the distribution of linguistic sounds are much more rigid than the rules regulating the distribution of paralinguistic sounds. If I intend to form the word "tin" I must produce the sounds "t," "i," and "n" exactly in that order and no other. However the rules regulating the distribution of paralinguistic sounds are much more flexible. For example, there are rules that regulate acceptable loudness for speaking in face-to-face conversations and when speaking over distances. However, these rules involve a range of options, and I can choose to speak with a variety of loudnesses in both the conversational or the distance situation. In other words, in the distribution of paralinguistic sounds, individual selection may play an important role since the individual has a wider range of options.

A major problem surrounding the delineation of language and paralanguage occurs in the articulation of words. Confusion arises from the fact that, in articulating language, certain types of sounds which are part of the phonemic system of language may have nothing to do with the phonemic system. There is universal agreement that coughs and sneezes are not language. However, in the case of vocal phenomena like pitch, loudness, rate, and duration, there are some differences among scholars as to differentiating the linguistic function of these phenomena from their non-linguistic function. For example, loudness is phonemic in English, which means it can perform the linguistic function of differentiating words like "permit" (the noun) and "permit" (the verb). However, a speaker can whisper these two words or shout them, the whisper and the shout being variations in loudness. In each case the speaker will have no difficulty understanding which word is the noun and which is the verb. This example demonstrates how the same physical phenomenon used to produce a speech sign, that is the force with which the air is expelled from the lungs, is at the same instant the basis of both phonemic differentiation (a linguistic necessity in English) and non-phonemic sound variation (a situational variation for speakers of English). This characteristic of loudness holds true for pitch, rate, and duration.

The presence or absence of paralinguistic features does not influence the denotative meaning of the words. For example, the word 'fire' is interpreted quite differently if said with extra high pitch and extreme loudness, in contrast to being said with normal pitch and normal loudness. The extreme or unusual use of pitch and loudness in no way alters the fact that 'fire' refers to the phenomenon of combustion manifested in light, flame, and heat.

Stating this point another way, there are many aspects of speech sign production that are not accounted for by linguistic analysis. These paralinguistic aspects of speaking are important for the study of semiotic psychology because such sounds often relate to important information regarding an individual's emotions and attitudes.

The following are several of items from a checklist in the *First Five Minutes* (Pittenger et al., 1960) that gives the reader an idea of the domain of behavior that is being referred to as paralanguage.

> A word or phrase broken off part way through and replaced by another, with or without hesitation. . . . the exact timing and the amount of delay before the replacement begins are important.
>
> Average conversational speech, . . . is not particularly smooth–it includes a good many hems and haws, stutters and corrections and abandoned phrases.
>
> Variations of volume, register, tempo and voice quality.
>
> Pauses, sighs, gasps, . . . (pp. 251–256).

At this stage of the scientific study of paralanguage it is helpful to have a method for unambiguously identifying the behavioral phenomena being investigated. It is also helpful to be able to distinguish the paralinguistic domain from other closely related areas of study. The purpose of the following diagrams and associated discussions is clarification of the domain of paralanguage.

Figure 5.1 is a model that indicates the most general case of communication involving two human beings.

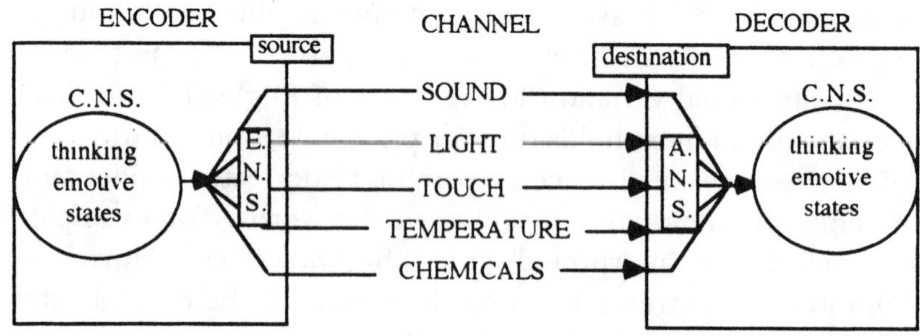

Figure 5.1

Definitions of the terms in Figure 5.1 are as follows:

Encoder = The originator of a message.

Decoder = The recipient of a message.

C.N.S. = The central nervous system; that is, the brain and spinal cord.

E.N.S. = The efferent nervous system; that is, nerve fibers carrying neural impulses from the C.N.S. to the muscles and glands.

A.N.S. = The afferent nervous system; that is, nerve fibers carrying neural impulses from sensory receptors to the C.N.S.

Source = A muscular movement, glandular secretion or biochemical change that originates a change in physical energy.

Destination = A sensory receptor that can respond to physical energy.

Channel = A medium that carries physical energy from encoders to decoders.

Figure 5.1 indicates that human communication takes place through the exchange of five types of physical energy: sound, light, touch, temperature, and chemistry. However, to unambiguously point to one particular channel of communication, it is necessary in technical discussions to specify more than the physical energy being exchanged between the speaker and the listener.

In the context of human communication, one could focus on the fact that sound is the physical energy involved for the speech channel and refer to this channel as *acoustic* communication. However, speakers may initiate acoustic communication by any one of a number of actions: snapping their fingers, tapping their foot, rocking their chair, and so on. The important technical information concerning these different means of activating a channel of communication is not that they all involve sound, it is that the source of the sound is the hand, foot, or torso.

The specification of the source of sound as the mouth is not sufficient to unambiguously identify the speech channel. One could, for example, specify the mouth as the source of physical energy and refer to this type of communication as *oral* communication. But the ear is not the only destination of changes in physical energy originated by the mouth. Movement of the mouth can be a stimulus for the eyes, and in kissing the destination is the body surface. From the standpoint of the scientific study of semiotic psychology, the important technical information is that the destination is the ear, eye, or body surface.

The channels of communication most closely related to speech sign behavior are: kinesics, odor, touch, observation, proxemics, and eye contact. Each of these channels–defined in terms of its source and destination–appears in Figure 5.2. Textbooks devoted to the topic of nonverbal communication provide information regarding the study of these channels (Burgoon, Buller, & Woodall, 1989; Knapp & Hall, 1992; Siegman & Feldstein, 1987). These textbooks also generally include discussions of paralinguistic phenomena, although the range of phenomena included and the labels applied to these phenomena vary among authors.

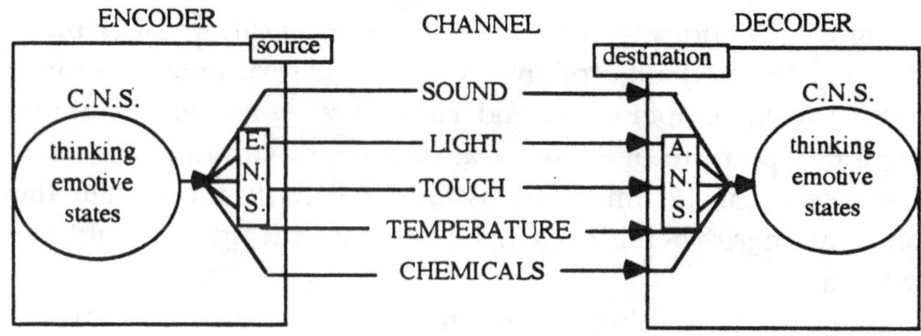

Figure 5.2

In terms of the exchange of physical energy, Figure 5.2 indicates how the speech channel differs from the other channels in two fundamental ways. First, the source of the physical energy on the speech channel is the vocal tract. Second, the destination of the physical energy initiated by the vocal tract is the ear.

The fundamental difference between the speech channel and the other channels is the fact that there are two codes on the speech channel. One code is linguistic and relates to the formation of words and the arrangement of these words into sentences. The second code is not related to the formation of words or their arrangement into sentences. This second code on the speech channel is *paralanguage*.

A final noteworthy point regarding the domain of paralanguage is the fact that it is always present when humans interact by way of language signs. The channels odor and touch are restricted to face-to-face communication. Kinesics, observation, proxemics, and eye contact are functional only when we can see the speaker. In contrast to these restrictions, the medium of transmission may be reduced to a telephone or a recording and the message will still contain paralanguage.

B. Sapir's Contribution

Sapir's 1927 article "Speech as a Personality Trait" provided the first programmatic statement for what was at a later date labeled paralanguage. In that article Sapir repeatedly emphasizes the distinction between the linguistic and paralinguistic aspects of speech.

At one point in the article he uses intonation to demonstrate the linguistic and paralinguistic aspects of speech stating that ". . . intonation has a twofold determination." Sapir describes the linguistic aspect of intonation as:

> Certain intonations which are a necessary part of our speech. If I say for example, 'Is he coming?' I raise the pitch of the voice on the last word. . . . It is one of the significant patterns of our English language to elevate the voice in interrogative sentences of a certain type, hence such elevation is not expressive in the properly individual sense of the word. . . .

In contrast, he emphasizes the paralinguistic aspect of intonation:

> But more than that, there is a second level . . . in intonation–the musical handling of the voice generally, quite aside from the properly linguistic patterns of intonation.

At another point in the article Sapir uses pronunciation as an example stating that "In pronunciation we again have to distinguish the social from the individual patterns." Sapir describes the linguistic aspect of pronunciation as:

> Society decrees that we pronounce certain selected consonants and vowels, which have been set aside as the bricks and mortar, as it were, for the construction of a given language. We cannot depart very widely from this decree.

Again to emphasize the contrast between language and paralanguage, Sapir spells out the paralinguistic aspect of pronunciation:

> But all the time there are also *individual* variations of sound which are highly important and which in many cases have a symptomatic value for the study of personality. (p. 902, emphasis in the original.)

The social science aspect of Sapir's article in general, and his identification of the paralinguistic aspects of speech sign behavior in particular, are noteworthy. First, throughout the article Sapir focuses on both particular and broad mental states which he surmised were revealed by an individual's language and paralanguage. A statement like "... unconsciously symbolic habits of articulation," indicates that Sapir had in mind the concept that observable speech signs are indexes of mental states. Second, his statements regarding paralinguistic phenomena were intended to provide a model for operational definitions of the myriad of speech sounds that accompany language rather than leaving the study of these important indicators of an individual's emotions and attitudes to intuition. In other words, in "Speech as a Personality Trait," Sapir intended to establish the study of semiotic psychology as a social science.

C. Trager's Taxonomy

George Trager was not the only one of Sapir's students to pursue his provocative thinking regarding the non-language aspect of speech;[1] however, he was the first to publish an elaborate expansion of Sapir's taxonomy (Trager, 1958).[2] Subsequently, Pittenger, Hockett, and Danehy expressly aimed to closely follow "Trager's classification and systemization of paralinguistic phenomena" in their their now classic work *The First Five Minutes* (Pittenger et al., 1960, p. 194). And since 1958, every review of the literature or textbook that covers the non-language aspect of speech refers to Trager's article "Paralanguage: A First Approximation."[3]

Trager first separates the non-language sounds into the categories of *voice set* and *paralanguage*. He refers to voice set as being prelinguistic defining it as a speaker's "physiological and physical peculiarities." He then defines paralanguage as consisting of *voice qualities*, which are modifications of both language and non-language sounds, and *vocalizations* which are non-language sounds. He makes no further elaboration regarding voice set other than to say that "the notation of voice set ... is then to be made in whatever ordinary descriptive terms are available, and to be understood as pre-analytic." Examples of such "ordinary descriptive terms" would be whether the speaker sounded old or young, healthy or sick, female or male, etc.

The following is Trager's taxonomy of paralanguage.

I. Voice Qualities

. . . modifications of all the language and other noises. [and] . . . overall or background characteristics of the voice . . . involve paired attributes but the pairs of terms are more properly descriptive of extremes between which there are continua or several intermittent degrees.

A. Pitch Range: Spread ↔ Narrowed
B. Vocal Lip Control: Rasp ↔ Openness
C. Glottis Control: Voicing ↔ Breathiness
D. Pitch Control: Sharp Transition ↔ Smooth Transition
E. Articulation Control: Forceful ↔ Relaxed
F. Articulation Placement: Projected ↔ Retracted
G. Rhythm Control: Smooth ↔ Jerky
H. Resonance: Resonant ↔ Thin
I. Tempo: Increased ↔ Decreased

II. Vocalizations

. . . variegated . . . noises, do not have the structure of language . . . actual specifically identifiable noises (sounds) or aspects of noises.

A. Vocal Characterizers

. . . a group of items whose number is yet not delimited, and which have a wide scope over or between linguistic material . . . may represent extremes of a continuum, something like the voice qualities; . . . with all of these one 'talks through' them.[4]

1. Laughing ↔ Crying (with giggling, snickering, whimpering, and sobbing in between);
2. Yelling ↔ Whispering (with muffled sounds and muttering in between);
3. Moaning ↔ Groaning;
4. Whining ↔ Breaking;
5. Belching ↔ Yawning;
6. ". . . and probably others . . ."

B. Vocal Qualifiers

. . . [also] have rather wide scope and may be combined with the [vocal] characterizers. . .

1. Intensity: overloud ↔ oversoft
2. Pitch Height: overhigh ↔ overlow
3. Extent: drawl ↔ clipping

C. Vocal Segregates

... sounds that are much like the sounds of language, but again differ from them in scope and concatenation ... (e.g., uh huh, tsk-tsk, brrr, etc.)

1. Segmental Sounds: recorded in a broad phonetic transcription
2. Silence ("zero-segregate")

Trager's taxonomy of the non-language aspect of speech is obviously related to the thinking of his mentor Sapir. Trager's particular contribution appears in the addition of highly specific operational definitions. These definitions provided the basis for employing paralinguistic transcriptions in a flurry of research projects which followed the publication of "Paralanguage: A First Approximation" (Siegman, 1978,1987).

PART III

SEMIOTIC PSYCHOLOGY

6

The Idiographic Paradigm

A. Introduction

1. The History of "The First Five Minutes"[1]

Between 1957 and 1960 the anthropological linguist Charles F. Hockett collaborated with two psychiatrists, Robert E. Pittenger and John J. Danehy, on a research project entitled "Linguistic-Psychiatric Analysis of Interview Samples."[2] The results of this project were published as *The First Five Minutes: A Sample of Microscopic Interview Analysis* (1960). The author's approach to the data and their definitions of the research problem were derived equally from anthropology, anthropological linguistics, and psychiatry. The authors also give credit to anthropologists, anthropological linguists and psychiatrists for providing the stimulus for the research project: Gregory Bateson, Ray L. Birdwhistell, Henry W. Brosin, Norman A. McQuown, Henry L. Smith, Jr., George Trager, and Frieda Fromm-Reichmann. The anthropological linguist on the project gives special credit to McQuown, Smith and Trager for having trained him in the techniques of paralinguistic transcription. Pittenger, Hockett and Danehy also indicate the importance of several previous publications that had explored the link between anthropological linguistics and psychiatry: Pittenger and Smith (1957), McQuown (1957), Pittenger (1958), and Eldred and Price (1958).

2. Mental States vs. Behavioral Signals

The purposes of the research project reported in *The First Five Minutes* were to gain knowledge about conversation in general and the psychiatric interview in particular. The selection of a psychiatric interview for microscopic analysis stemmed from

Pittenger, Hockett, and Danehy's interest in the practical application of linguistics to psychiatry; specifically, the training of new psychotherapists. They point out that psychiatrists are trained to identify *mental states*, such as 'anger,' but are not trained to detect *behavioral signals*, such as 'loudness,' which are the observable behaviors from which psychiatrists infer the *mental state* of 'anger.' The difference between a *mental state* and a *behavioral signal* can be illustrated by considering the difference between an inference about the motivation of a speaker: "he's a male chauvinist," and a description of that speaker's behavior: "he's always interrupting me."

In the usual course of events an interlocutor does not describe the linguistic and paralinguistic behavior that occurs in a conversation. If asked to describe a conversation, interlocutors, e.g., psychotherapists, will state inferences regarding what they have heard. However, conscious awareness of the physical characteristics of speech sounds is an invaluable aid to an interlocutor–psychotherapist or any other–who is concerned about the emotions or attitudes of his or her conversational partner. For example, before other more obvious clues might appear, an increase in loudness might alert a concerned interlocutor to the presence of anger, be it his or her own or the person's with whom he or she is conversing. Similarly, the primary purpose of Pittenger, Hockett, and Danehy is to determine how a speaker's language and paralanguage correlates with a psychiatrist's description of the emotions and attitudes of that speaker.

A linguistic and paralinguistic transcription of a conversation, that is, a microscopic analysis, involves an enormous amount of time, which was the rationale for Pittenger, Hockett, and Danehy selecting only five minutes for analysis. They report that the linguistic and paralinguistic transcription of these five minutes of conversation required between twenty-five and thirty hours; a minimum of five hours was needed to transcribe one minute of conversation! A brief excerpt of their transcription appears in the Methods section, below.

The five-minute conversation analyzed in *The First Five Minutes* is the first five minutes of an initial psychiatric interview that was reported and discussed in the book *The Initial Interview in Psychiatric Practice* (Gill, Newman, & Redlich, 1956).

Pittenger, Hockett, and Danehy provide the following reason for choosing this particular sample ". . . it is an initial interview, and the patient is an outpatient. We thought it might be more interesting and revealing . . . to examine the opening gambits of two people who have never met before than to try to understand some comparably brief episode deep in the middle of an extensive course of therapy, when the participants have already established a host of special conventions and mutual understandings." Another major reason given is: ". . . the interview takes place in a setting, and with the kinds of aims, that are characteristic of psychiatric practice in general."

From a scientific point of view the most important reason the authors give for selecting this particular conversational sample is that copies are easily available to any interested investigator because a phonograph record containing these five minutes accompanies the book *The Initial Interview in Psychiatric Practice*. The availability of the phonograph record means the data on which the conclusions are based can be verified by other investigators. In the scientific community this aspect of research is called *reliability*, which for PHD means: " . . . [O]ur reactions, as presented herein, can be independently checked by any reader who wishes to. The evidence on which our inferences are based is just the evidence available to anyone who listens to the recording" (p. 7).

3. An Idiographic Project

The research philosophy of the *The First Five Minutes* is distinctly different from that of *The Study of Spontaneous Talk* described in the following chapter. Pittenger, Hockett, and Danehy state that their approach to science is "idiographic" rather than "nomothetic." The authors cite the work of Gordon W. Allport (1942) as a source of an outstanding explication of the distinction between nomothetic and idiographic research philosophies. The distinction between nomothetic and idiographic research is that in a nomothetic study the investigator is interested in general tendencies, laws, or in making statements about "normal" behavior that characterizes a group. In an idiographic study the investigator is interested in the particular and unique, in making statements that characterize an individual.

Ultimately, what differentiates the Pittenger, Hockett, and Danehy study from those reported in the following chapters is the difference in the manner in which the *raw data*, that is, the recorded conversation, was analyzed. First, the two psychiatrists drew inferences about the motivational and emotive states of the speaker from the linguist's transcription of language and paralanguage. Second, the two psychiatrists drew inferences about the motivational and emotive states of the speaker by listening to the recording, and the anthropological linguist looked for the specific linguistic and paralinguistic signals that could have been the basis of their inferences. Pittenger, Hockett and Danehy state that this approach is *idiographic* rather than *nomothetic* in that they were primarily interested in answering questions such as: What do these two interlocutors say? Why do they say it? How do they say it? What is the impact of what is being said on these two interlocutors? What is being communicated unconsciously between these two interlocutors? How does the orientation of these two interlocutors change during the conversation? In other words, Pittenger, Hockett and Danehy were not interested in comparing this conversation to other conversations, or these interlocutors to other interlocutors. Had they been concerned with such comparisons, they would have had to transcribe many more conversations with other interlocutors. That method would have made their study nomothetic rather than idiographic.

B. Methods

1. Description of Subjects

Information about the patient in the conversation was obtained from the book *The Initial Interview in Psychiatric Practice* (Gill et al., 1956) where it is reported that: "A thirty-year old married woman telephoned the Clinic and asked for an appointment. She was seen four days later" (p. 113).

The only available information about the psychiatrist in the conversation is supplied by Pittenger, Hockett, and Danehy, ". . . the therapist is experienced, not a beginner. We wanted something typical of good therapy, not something illustrative of the difficulties the beginner is apt to encounter" (p. 7).

2. Recording Techniques

Information about the recording procedure employed was also obtained from the book *The Initial Interview in Psychiatric Practice* (Gill, Newman & Redlich, 1956), where the recording situation was described as follows:

> These recordings were made in a special room. The room is approximately nine by eleven feet and has no windows. The size and shape of its walls, floors, and ceiling, and the furnishings and materials were planned for acoustic excellence. It is furnished more like a conventional small waiting room than an office: there is no desk but a round table, two comfortable upholstered chairs and a couch. Along one wall is a one-way mirror. In the wall are ducts for the air-conditioning equipment. The room has an average noise level of 35 decibels. In it one hears no outside noise and one's own voice sounds quite natural. The microphone is concealed in the lamp on the table. The recording equipment is in an adjacent room. The microphone is an Altec Lansing 21B Miniature Condenser and the recording machine is an Ampex Model 300 tape recorder. This setup, the room and the electrical equipment, meet the need for a high fidelity recording unit. The unit enables one to make records that can be heard with ease and eliminates the strain and fatigue of listening to acoustically poor recordings. Such recordings give a true facsimile of what was said and how it was said in the interview, of every intonation of voice, sigh, mutter, murmur, or silence. (pp. 114–115)

3. Coding Language and Paralanguage

The "microscopic analysis," that is, the linguistic and paralinguistic transcription of the conversation, was accomplished by the anthropological linguist on the project, Charles F. Hockett. Although the raw data on which the results of a particular study are based are not typically reported in a psychological research article, a paraphrase of *The First Five Minutes* would be greatly remiss by not indicating to some extent what such a microscopic analysis looks like, since Pittenger, Hockett, and Danehy devote approximately one-third of their book to this transcription. In addition, another entire chapter is devoted to explaining the conventions of the linguistic and paralinguistic transcriptions. I have therefore included a brief sample of the linguistic and paralinguistic transcription, and following it, a description of the transcription conventions that occur in this brief sample. This sample is the very opening of the conversation, for which a typical conversational transcription would be:

Therapist: Will you sit there? What brings you here?
Patient: Everything's wrong. I get so irritable, tense, depressed. Just everything and everybody gets on my nerves.
Therapist: Yeah.

At this point I would like to suggest that it might help the reader understand the heuristic point of Pittenger, Hockett, and Danehy if this transcript is read again imagining that you are hearing it from the recording of the conversation. After becoming familiar with the linguistic and paralinguistic analysis below, go back and 'listen' again to the conversation. The basic point of *The First Five Minutes* is the benefits of increased sensitivity to language and paralanguage, and this exercise should demonstrate the effects of such consciousness raising to the reader.

Microscopic Analysis:

4:
3: Ø H: Ø
2: hwət+briŋz+yuw+hihr#
1: [T1a] Will you sit there? [T1b] What brings you here? (35) [P1a] (5)

4: LD_{11}–LD_{11} SQ- -SQ
RG_{11}- LD_{s2}- -LD_{s2}
3: du_{d1} du_{c1}ʔ Ø ʔ Ø Ø
2: evriy+θiŋ+z+ rɔŋ| ay+get+so ihrɨtɨbl|| tens|
1: Everything's wrong. [P1b] I get so (30) irritable, (10) tense, (10)

4: SQ–SQ SQ- -SQ SQ–SQ
-RG_{11}
3: Ø
2: diprest# jɨst+evrθiŋɨn+ evrɨbədiy | gets+an+may+nəhrvz#
1: depressed. (40) [P1c] Just everything and everybody gets on my nerves.

4: LD_{s1}-LD_{s1}
NS-NS
3: Ø du_{c1}
2: yeh#
1: (10) [T2]Yeah.

Explanation of the Linguistic and Paralinguistic Transcription.[3]

Line 1. Line 1 contains the ordinary spelling of the usual transcription, but in addition, the conversation has been segmented into *turns*. The therapist's turns are indicated by 'T' and the patient's by 'P.' The turns are then numbered consecutively with Arabic numerals (1, 2, 3). Within turns lowercase letters (a,b,c) were added by Pittenger, Hockett, and Danehy to aid in citing specific parts of the longer turns.

Also, Pittenger, Hockett, and Danehy have recorded the duration of silent pauses on Line 1 by numbers in parentheses. The numbers indicate the duration of the silent pause in tenths of a second.

Line 2. Line 2 is a phonemic transcription of the conversation. In a phonemic transcription there is a one-to-one correspondence between the orthographic symbols and the sounds being produced. For example, in [P1a] the interlocutor says a word which in ordinary spelling is written 'wrong.' However, in saying this word the speaker produced only three sounds: r, ɔ and ŋ. The special symbols ɔ and ŋ are needed to maintain the principle that one sound is equal to one symbol. In the spelling 'ng' two symbols indicate what is only one sound. The 'ɔ' is needed because the letter of the English alphabet 'o' can be pronounced in several different ways: 'women,' 'box,' 'note' and 'son.' In none of these words would a native speaker of English use the same sound that is used in the word 'wrong.' The vowel and consonant phonemes together are *segmental phonemes*.

In addition to the segmental vowel and consonant phonemes like r, ɔ and ŋ, there are also the *suprasegmental phonemes* of pitch, loudness,[4] and juncture. Pitch phonemes are not included at all in this brief sample, and the only loudness phoneme included is primary, which is indicated by an underline. So, for example in [T1b] the phonemic transcription indicates that the speaker put the greatest amount of loudness in that sentence on the word "here." This transcription convention is necessary because every English sentence has one primary loudness phoneme, but ordinary spelling offers no way to indicate where in the sentence the speaker places the primary loudness phoneme.

The suprasegmental phonemic junctures are indicated in ordinary spelling by commas, periods, question marks, and exclamation points. However, these symbols do not always refer to exactly the same vocal phenomena. For this reason the symbols +, |, || and # are used to indicate the actual vocal phenomena that a speaker produces between words (+), at the end of a phrase (|), the rise in pitch at the end of question sentences (||), and the fall in pitch that occurs at the end of statement-of-fact sentences (#). The '+' indicates the ordinary transition between words like 'night rate.' Compare to 'nitrate,' which is exactly the same sequence of consonant and vowel phonemes as in 'night rate,' but lacks the + juncture. The '|' is fairly consistently equivalent to the comma. '||' represents a rise in pitch that very often is reflected in ordinary spelling by a question mark. '#' is approximately equivalent to a period. The necessity of this phonemic alphabet is apparent in the brief sample presented above. In [T1b] "What brings you here?" is a question, but does not end in the rising pitch that accompanies a 'vocal question mark.' On the other hand, in [P1b] the word "irritable" is pronounced with a rising pitch, or a 'vocal question mark.' Also, in [P1c], the spelling indicates two words "everything and." However, in the actual pronunciation by P there was no 'space' between the "everything" and the "and." For this reason there is no + at this point in the phonemic transcription.

Line 3. Line 3 is the first level of the paralinguistic transcription. The phenomena recorded on Line 3 are *vocal segregates.* The vocal segregates occurring in the brief sample are 1) Ø, 2) H, 3) :, 4) ʔ, 5) du_{d1} and 6) $du_{c1.}$ These symbols refer to: 1) silent pause, 2) audible glottal friction without voicing, 3) increased duration, 4) glottal closure, 5) one degree of drawl, and 6) one degree of clipping.

Line 4. Line 4 is the second level of paralinguistic transcription, *voice qualities.* These are vocal phenomena that are two or more phonemes in duration. In contrast to the vocal segregates, which are either single sounds or modifications of single sounds, the voice qualities modify entire words, sentences or paragraphs. The voice qualities in the brief sample are 1) RG_{11}, 2) $LD_{11,}$ 3) SQ, 4) LD_{s2} and 5) NS, which respectively symbolize 1) slight overlow pitch, 2) slight overloud, 3) squeeze,[5] 4) considerable oversoft, and 5) nasalization.

C. Results

1. Segmental Phonemes

As indicated, the format of *The First Five Minutes* is different from the format of other social psychological research studies stemming from the fact that the research is idiographic rather than nomothetic. There is no Results section in which the authors employ statistics, either descriptive or inferential. For Pittenger, Hockett, and Danehy, results are the emotive and motivational states of the interlocutors inferred by the psychiatrists from the linguistic and paralinguistic signals transcribed by the anthropological linguist, and these inferences are continuous throughout the chapter "Transcription and Analysis," to which one-half of the book is devoted. The following is a sample of this transcription and analysis.

The focus is on "irritable" in [P1b].

> We are unable to account for the unusual pronunciation of "irritable," with /ihr-/[6] in place of the normal /ir-/. Yet even a wild guess is perhaps worth registering. The pronunciation P uses might be a subliminal pun with "ear," which in her dialect would be /ihr/. Would this be a suggestion that it is via hearing that P chiefly receives irritating stimuli?

2. Suprasegmental Phonemes

The focus is on [T1b]: "What brings you here#."

> If T had said "What brings you here" changing nothing but the location of the primary stress (on you instead of here), emphasis would have been on the particular patient in contrast to other people, and could have been interpreted as implying disapproval or surprise that this patient had gotten into the sort of trouble that other people do.
>
> Another possible intonation would be "What brings you here ||." This would seem much more animated, thus bring T and his emotions and personality more emphatically into the picture. If we may assume that T wishes to avoid this, then the intonation he chooses is much better.

3. Vocal Segregates

The focus is on [P1b]:

ʔ Ø ʔ Ø Ø

"I get so (30) irritable|| (10) tense| (10) depressed#"

> [P1b] shows unmistakable signs of 'rehearsal.' In anticipating the interview, P has planned certain things that she is going to say, and now simply reads this one off from memory. . . . The pause (∅) with glottal closure (ʔ) after 'so,' and then the spacing-out of the three adjectives, the first two with non-final intonations and the third with a distinctly final one, are reminiscent of 'dramatic reading,' and not characteristic of ordinary conversation.

4. Voice Qualities

The focus is on [P1a, b & c]:

LD_{11}–LD_{11} SQ- -SQ
RG_{11}- LD_{s1}–LD_{s2}
[P1a] Everything's wrong. [P1b] I get so irritable, tense,
SQ-SQ SQ-
-RG_{11}
depressed. [P1c] Just
-SQ SQ–SQ
everything and everybody gets on my nerves.

> The features of voice quality on [P1a] and [P1c] show that those are not in any way intended as diagnostic or etiological accompaniments to the statement of P's complaint in [P1b]. Rather, they constitute an incipient and partial *demonstration* to T of the manner in which P acts out her irritation, tension, and depression. . . . It will also be noticed that [P1a-b] and [P2c] differ in manner of delivery: the former is slightly overlow throughout, and markedly oversoft on "I get so;" the latter is not overlow . . . [these] are hints of the style of 'whining complaint' . . . The oversoft and squeeze on 'I get so' conceal the words to the point that, in the transcript in the book *The Initial Interview* they are rendered as 'I guess.' We must allow for the possibility that T hears the phrase thus, or otherwise perceives it incorrectly. (pp. 24–26, emphases in the original.)

D. Discussion

One conclusion of Pittenger, Hockett, and Danehy is that *The First Five Minutes* demonstrates that psychiatric inferences about emotive states are not figments of psychiatrists' imaginations; quite the contrary, these inferences are based on observable behavior that can be studied scientifically.

> We are impelled by our experience in the present project to propose that a state of a person is not, after all, something hidden inside, insusceptible to direct observation. Rather, it is some contour or pattern of

> the person's totality of communicative behavior. . . . The linguist has names and symbols for individual items; the psychiatrist has names for the whole Gestalts. This view frees the psychiatrist from any accusation of mysticism or magic. (p. 245)

A major extrapolation of this conclusion is that language and paralanguage not only provide the scientific basis for psychiatric inferences, but are observable behaviors that operationally define 'mind.' The implication is that saying that we know what is 'on a person's mind' means that we are familiar with that person's linguistic and paralinguistic habits. Another conclusion of Pittenger, Hockett, and Danehy is that their research points to the importance of microscopic signals in indicating the boundary-markers in the hierarchical nature and developmental structure of conversations. Pittenger, Hockett, and Danehy define boundary-markers as the linguistic and paralinguistic signals by which interlocutors indicate to each other that one segment of the conversation has ended and that another segment is to begin. The segments indicated by boundary-markers may be of brief or long duration, but they are all essential in determining accurately the developmental structure of a conversation. Furthermore, Pittenger, Hockett, and Danehy state that certain linguistic and paralinguistic signals cannot be understood or interpreted as being anything else but boundary-markers.

The developmental structure of a conversation is hierarchical. That is in the course of a conversation there are changes in topic and the mental states. Within segments of discussing a particular topic or expressing a particular emotion, there are minor shifts in emphasis. All changes and shifts, major or minor, are signaled by linguistic and paralinguistic boundary-markers. These relatively microscopic signals are crucial for the analysis of conversation as a social psychological process.

This second point, the importance of linguistic and paralinguistic signals as indicators of major developmental divisions in a conversation, is tempered by Pittenger, Hockett, and Danehy's discussion of a serious danger of microscopic analysis. This danger is missing the gestalt of the entire conversation by focusing too intently on single microscopic linguistic and paralinguistic signals. It is the problem of the "forest and the trees." In this instance the intense concentration on one microscopic event can easily distort its significance. Furthermore, in different contexts the same microscopic event may have different significance. For Pittenger, Hockett, and Danehy, the way to avoid such distortion is to understand a conversation as a developmental process in which a microscopic event may play a relatively minor role at one stage, for example signaling a change in topic, or a major role, for example signaling the termination of the interaction. In other words, the importance of a microscopic event is determined by its function in pointing to a particular hierarchical segment that plays a role in the developmental structure of a conversation.

7

The Nomothetic Paradigm

A. Introduction

This research was originally reported by Soskin and John as a chapter in the book *The Stream of Behavior* (1963). At the time they wrote this research report, William F. Soskin was a Research Associate in the Department of Psychiatry of Harvard University, and Vera P. John was an Assistant Professor in the Department of Anthropology and Sociology at the University of Rochester. Their research efforts were supported by a Public Health Service Research grant awarded by the National Institute of Mental Health. Soskin and John describe their work as "a program of research on person-environment interaction as revealed in the analysis of spontaneous talk," which they pursued to discover "the means by which humans achieve, maintain, relieve, or avoid certain internal states." Their aim was to identify the relationship between the linguistic performance of interlocutors in conversations as either a stimulus for, or a response to, modifications in the social environment. This goal, generalizing their work into the much larger domain of "the psychology of social roles," of which conversation is a part, might seem to be seriously compromised by the fact that this research is based solely on speech channel data. However, Soskin and John point out that, although the other channels of communication (e.g., kinesics, proxemics, eye-contact, etc.) do carry important information for the expression of social roles, that "an overwhelmingly large part of the information relevant to interpersonal relations is carried by the verbal message alone" (p. 235). Furthermore, the authors emphasize that sequential recordings of conversations over time are prime sources for understanding how individuals manage intrapsychic states through the linguistic management of their relations with their social environment.

B. Methods

1. Description of Subjects

The results of this study are based on the conversations of a young couple who had been married for about one year. The woman was a college graduate, and the man was a graduate student at the time the study took place. The woman was 20 years of age and the man 25. The major consideration in the selection of the subjects was their ability to carry with them in plain sight a microphone and recording pack and to be able to carry this live microphone for 16 hours a day. The main inducement for the subjects to volunteer to participate was the offer of a free vacation at a very pleasant summer resort, which was the site of the project.

2. Recording Techniques

The subjects' conversations were recorded by means of a miniature radio transmitter worn by the subjects. These transmitters were sensitive enough to pick up both the subjects' utterances and those of their interlocutors. The radio transmitter output was tape-recorded at a radio receiving station. The transmitter was a small gray metal box about 1.5 inches x 2.5 inches x 5 inches in overall dimension, with a roughly foot-long antenna protruding from the upper end. This box was mounted high on the shoulder strap of a camera case, and in wearing position it hung behind the shoulder blade with the antenna clearly visible. An inch-square microphone was mounted high on the front part of the shoulder strap, the wires from which led along the strap to the transmitter and down to the case containing a mercury-cell power supply. The entire unit weighed about three pounds, and could be worn comfortably for several hours.

3. Instructions to Subjects

The subjects were informed that there was no expectation of them other than that they provide the research group the opportunity to record their conversations, and to regard themselves as on vacation. In the weeks preceding going to the camp grounds, Dr. Soskin held several talks with the subjects during which he gave them a full and detailed understanding of the objectives and relevance of the study. The subjects were also informed of the provisions made for safeguarding their anonymity in the processing of data and in eventual publication of the results.

4. The Context

The summer resort consisted of approximately 500 adults and children, mostly family groups, and approximately 50 college students who worked on the grounds in various capacities. The subjects lived in a small cottage at the edge of a very large lake. The locus of activity of the resort was a rectangular area about a mile in length and about a half-mile wide. The receiving station, where the radio transmissions were tape-recorded, was situated on the edge of a bluff above the camp grounds. The receiving station building was a small structure shielded from the camp grounds by a dense growth of trees.

The basic units for the description of the social and psychological context in which the conversations occurred were the *episode* and the *phase* (Barker & Wright, 1955; Barker, 1960). The episode is "an organized sequence of behaviors occurring within a specifiable locale and devoted to a particular activity. The episode may be of varying duration, may be interrupted periodically by intervening episodes, may involve the subject with different individuals at different times, etc." (p. 250). In the present study an entire 16-hour day of the behavior of the male subject was analyzed into episodes. An ecological description of one of these episodes, the "Rowing Episode" is as follows:

> The recording is from the first hour of the first morning that 'Roz' (the wife) and 'Jock' (the husband) wore the transmitters. Shortly before, on this beautifully sunny late-June morning, they had been sitting on the grass with the principal investigator while he reviewed again the general program and objectives of the pilot run, explained the various features of the living arrangements in what was to them a completely strange environment, and initiated them in the intricacies of the care and wearing of the transmitter. After the investigator departed, Roz and Jock set off to explore the waterfront. 'Tess,' with whom they are talking as the episode begins, is the wife of the radio operator. . . . As this episode begins, Jock and Roz are down at the swimming pier talk-

> ing to Tess before going rowing. [They then rented a boat and the episode covers the time that they were on the lake rowing in the boat]. (pp. 235-236)

5. Phase Analysis

Any performance analysis that lumps together the data from a series of episodes, or even one that summarizes one long episode, is in danger of obscuring many of the subtle aspects of conversation that occur within an episode. To study these changes in performance within episodes, *phases* of the episode are identified. Phases are organized sequences of behavior occurring within episodes. The rowing episode described above, for example, was divided by Soskin and John into five approximately distinct phases as follows:

Phase #1: the interval in which Jock seemed to be playfully showing off his skill as an oarsman;
Phase #2: the period in which Roz diffidently undertook to learn to row;
Phase #3: the encounter with the motor boat and ferry boat;
Phase #4: the aftermath of the scare during which both were rather angry and argumentative until Jock's easy laughter and change of mood in [unit] #215;
Phase #5: the remainder of the ride up to the point at which they left the dock.

6. Quantitative Performance

Quantitative performance refers to the absolute and relative amounts of talking time occurring in conversations. In any analysis of conversation a unit of analysis has to be identified, and in this study Soskin and John identify their unit of analysis as "the time interval during which S is judged to be talking. It may consist of a word, a phrase, or several sentences, and may project beyond the actual production of sound, when content, intonation or context indicate that S is still 'claiming' the available talking time" (p. 251). The authors then developed the following quantitative measures of talking time:

1. Total talking time (TTT): the sum of durations of the units produced by all the participants in a particular episode. TTT

may not exceed the clocked duration of the episode itself, hence, overlapping units are scored simply as time in use.

2. Demand for talking time (D): TTT as a proportion of the clocked duration of the episode.
3. Subject talking time (STT): the sum of the durations of the units of the subject's speech in a given episode.
4. Subject's proportion of TTT (S%): the proportion STT÷ TTT.

To facilitate the measurement procedures, the tape-recordings of the conversations were played through a graphic level recorder that electronically transformed the speech on the tape-recordings by way of inked pens onto a paper tape that moved under the pens. As a reliability check on this method, the same 45-minute sample was analyzed on two different occasions four months apart by the same person. For 107 units, there was 96 percent agreement on the definition of the units and a correlation of .98 between the two sets of graphic level recorder measurements (Hargreaves, 1955).

7. Content Performance

Soskin and John state that their content analysis technique was developed by their "own examination of spontaneous utterance, leavened by the work of Morris (1946); Ogden and Richards (1947); Piaget (1920); and, Skinner (1957)" (pp. 253–254). Their resulting content analysis coded six categories of content.

1. Exclamations. Soskin and John refer to this category of content as *expressive statements*. These are utterances such as (a) Ouch! (b) Wow! (c) Darn! (d) Gosh!
2. Thinking Aloud. Soskin and John refer to this category of content as *excogitive statements*. These are the verbal acts commonly described as "talking to oneself." The following, if imagined as spoken to the self, are representative: (a) Hmm, let me see. (b) Oh, let's see. (c) I guess you can't really predict. (d) I wonder if it would work this way. (e) I think what we're talking about is power.
3. Subjective Reports. Soskin and John refer to this category of content as *signones*. These statements report the speaker's

physical or psychological state, and therefore make available otherwise private information. They include reports on physical sensations, emotional dispositions, needs, hopes, wishes, likes and dislikes, etc. Examples are: (a) I'm cold, tired, hungry, etc. (b) I'm afraid, disappointed, angry, thrilled, etc. (c) I wish I could go; I hope you'll be able to come. (d) It was a very awkward time for me. (e) I now find it difficult to trust people.

4. Objective Reports. Soskin and John refer to this category of content as *structones.* These informational statements report facts, identify, classify, analyze, explain, etc. In contrast to subjective reports, objective reports have a validity independent of the personal experience of the speaker. Examples are: (a) I weigh 181 pounds. (b) That fits over the axle. (c) He was here yesterday. (d) I saw the two of them laughing. (e) I coach the soccer team. (f) The people I hang out with don't talk about that.
5. Judgments. Soskin and John refer to this category of content as *metrones.* These are evaluative statements arising out of the speaker's belief system, or his [/her] interpretation of his [/her] environment. Examples are: (a) Yours is the best one here. (b) It seems to occur most frequently amongst the female population. (c) She was more friendly than usual. (d) I think that sucks. (e) It tends to be for personal gain.
6. Persuasion. Soskin and John refer to this category of content as *regones.*

These are regulative statements such as demands, prohibitions, requests, etc., but also invitations, permissions and suggestions. For example: (a) Why don't you do it right now? (b) Won't you join us? (c) Of course, as you know. (d) That generalization is not always true. (e) Do you want me to give an example or a definition.

C. Results

1. Quantitative Performance

Table 7.1 shows the results of the quantitative measurement of Jock's linguistic performance in five different episodes. These

Jock's Qualitative Performance in Five Episodes

	Episode	Number of Interlocutors Present	Duration in Minutes	D[a]	S%[b]
1.	Breakfast	4	38	.93	36
2.	Lunch	4	35	.85	36
3.	Packing with Roz	2	29	.33	45
4.	Planning with Roz	2	16	.25	69
5.	Discussion with Research Assistant	2	14	.94	37

[a]D = Demand for talking time.
[b]S% = Jock's percentage of the talking time

Table 7.1

include two four-interlocutor episodes while seated at mealtime (Breakfast and Lunch), and three two-interlocutor episodes with his wife in the cabin (Planning and Packing). The fifth episode is a discussion with one of the research assistants.

In both of the four-interlocutor episodes, talking was the predominant activity (D), consuming 93 percent of the time in the Breakfast episode and 85 percent in the Lunch episode. In both instances Jock consumed 36 percent of the talking time (S%). If the other three interlocutors in the two four-interlocutor episodes were to divide the remaining time equally, they would have been able to speak only a little more than half as long as Jock.

In contrast with the four-interlocutor episodes, demand for talking time (D) was low in the two episodes with Roz, the Planning episode and the Packing episode. However, Jock's percentage of talking time was greater in episodes with his wife alone than in any other episode in which others were present (S%). In the Planning episode it was twice as large as in the Breakfast and Lunch episodes. In the third two-interlocutor episode, the discussion with the research assistant, the demand for talking time (D) was as high as in the Breakfast and Lunch episodes. However, in this episode Jock's proportion of the total talking time (D) was only 37 percent, less than his share if the total talking time was divided equally between the two interlocutors.

2. Content Performance

The distribution of 1,861 content categories spoken by Roz in five episodes and by Jock in six episodes, covering a span of three different days, indicates the overall occurrence of the different content categories

Table 7.2 indicates the overall percentages for the occurrence of the content categories used by Roz in five different episodes with her husband, and those used by Jock in six episodes–the last one not involving his wife. Table 7.2 indicates no significant difference in the overall use of the Excogitive, Signone, and Metrone content categories. The use of the Excogitive content category was, in fact, very rare, neither subject using this category more than one percent of the time. Roz produced significantly more Expressive content (p <.001). Jock used significantly more Regone and Structone content categories (p <.05 and p <.001, respectively).

The percentages for the use of the content categories in the five different episodes are shown in Table 7.3. The first column of Table 7.3 indicates that Roz produced a significantly higher percentage of Expressive content than did her husband in both

The Over-All Use of the Content Categories[a]

Content Categories	Roz's Percent[b]	Jock's Percent[c]	t	*p*
Expressive	9	4	4.85	< .001
Excogitive	1	1	0.67	NS
Signone	28	24	1.85	NS
Metrone	27	26	0.45	NS
Regone	11	14	2.05	< .05
Structone	25	31	3.40	< .001

[a]Based on 5 episodes for Roz and 6 for Jock.
[b]N = 745
[c]N = 1,116

Table 7.2

Percent Usage of the Content Categories in 5 Episodes

Episode	Subject	Express	Excogit.	Signone	Metro.	Regone	Struct.
1. Cabin	Roz	13[*,a]	1	29[b]	23	15[b]	19[a]
	Jock	3	2	27[y]	24[y]	19[y]	25[y]
2. Rowing	Roz	13[*,a]	2	32[*,b]	32	11[b]	11[a]
	Jock	7	0	17[y]	25[y]	33[*,y]	18[*,y]
3. Craft-Shop	Roz	1[b]	1	31[b]	30[x]	10[b]	27[b]
	Jock	2	2	41[x]	20[*,y]	18[y]	18[y]
4. Lunch	Roz	1[b]	0	24[b]	22	8[b]	44[b]
	Jock	2	0	23[y]	24[y]	5[*]	46
5. Break-fast	Roz	1[b]	0	13[a]	30	2[a]	54[b]
	Jock	1	0	18[y]	25[x]	2[x]	44[x]

* = Significant difference between subjects, $p < .005$.
a,b = Significant difference for Roz within a content category, $p < .05$. Not significant between numbers with the same letter.
x,y = Significant difference for Jock within a content category, $p < .05$. Not significant between numbers with the same letter.

Table 7.3

the Cabin episode and the Rowing episode (p <.05). Roz's percentage of output of Expressive content in the two interlocutor episodes was significantly greater than in the group or public situations (Craft Shop, Lunch and Breakfast, (p <.05).

Table 7.3 indicates that the 13 percent Signone usage by Roz in the Breakfast episode is significantly lower than that observed in any other episode (p <.05). Her use of Signones was significantly greater than Jock's in the Rowing episode (p <.05). Jock produced relatively fewer Signones in the Breakfast episode, about the same proportion as he produced in the Rowing episode (p <.05). But, his 41 percent in the Craft Shop is significantly higher than his output in any other episode.

Metrones were produced by Roz in each of the episodes at a rate between 22 and 32 percent for all content categories, and there is no significant difference for her between episodes. Jock's spread is somewhat larger, from 20 per cent in the Craft Shop episode to 35 per cent in the Breakfast episode. Jock's 35 percent in the Breakfast episode is significantly greater than that for any other episode except the Rowing episode (p <.05). His lowest production of Metrones was in the Craft Shop episode, which was also significantly lower than Roz's use of this content category in this episode (p <.005).

Both Roz and Jock produced significantly more Regones in their private interactions (Cabin and Rowing) than when in the presence of others (Craft Shop, Breakfast and Lunch). Roz's output of Regones in the breakfast episode was significantly lower than in any other episode (p <.05). For Jock there was no statistically significant difference in Regone percents between the Breakfast and Lunch episodes, but his output in these episodes was significantly lower than in the other episodes (p <.05). In the Rowing episode Jock's Regone percentage was significantly higher than his wife's (p <.005).

Roz's 11 percent for Structones in the Rowing episode and 19 percent in the Cabin episode were significantly lower than the percents observed for her in any other episode (p <.05). Both for her and for her husband the highest percentage of Structones appeared in the dining hall conversations, and these percents were significantly higher than those observed in all other episodes (p <.05). A significant difference between subjects in the use of Structones occurred in the Rowing episode (p <.005).

Table 7.4 indicates the percentage of occurrences of the content categories in the five phases of the Rowing episode. These phases are described in the Methods section, above. Figure 7.1 portrays graphically these percentages. The graphs make clear that the distribution of the four content categories that occurred with any frequency changes markedly for the two subjects at different phases in the episode. Roz's output of Regones was uniformly low throughout. Her output of Signones and Metrones dropped markedly in Phase 3, then gradually returned to the former level in Phases 4 and 5. Her use of Structones, on the other hand, rose precipitously in Phase 3, then gradually subsided again. For Jock the output of Regones, already high in Phase 1, climbed progressively higher throughout the next two phases and reached a peak in the tense minutes of Phase 3 when it seemed likely that the boat might be

Percent Content Categories in 5 Phases of the Rowing Episode

Phase	Subject	Signones	Metrones	Regones	Structones
1	Roz	33	36	15	9
	Jock	27	15	23	19
2	Roz	45	24	10	7
	Jock	21	26	37	16
3	Roz	19	14	10	38
	Jock	3	23	53	3
4	Roz	35	35	10	20
	Jock	7	34	45	14
5	Roz	29	32	9	13
	Jock	19	28	23	24

Table 7.4

swamped. From then on, Regone output subsided, and for both subjects there was a fairly high frequency of Metrones.

D. Discussion

1. Quantitative Performance

Soskin and John point out that the quantitative measures of linguistic performance portray Jock as very garrulous in some circumstances, though less so in others. Over a relatively large sample of situations he speaks about as much as his interlocutors. However, given an appropriate audience he appeared quite ready to take the initiative and to claim considerably more than his share of talking time. Jock's quantitative performance was also characterized by a disproportional large use of the available talking time. Roz, too, showed herself to be a fairly spontaneous person in social situations. However, she was much more sensitive both to her own impact on the group and to the possible interests and needs of other group members than Jock.

2. Content Performance

The statistical description of the subjects' content performance is the basis of several inferences. Evidently in Phase #1, Roz was relatively free in providing information about her own internal

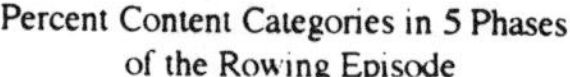

Figure 7.1

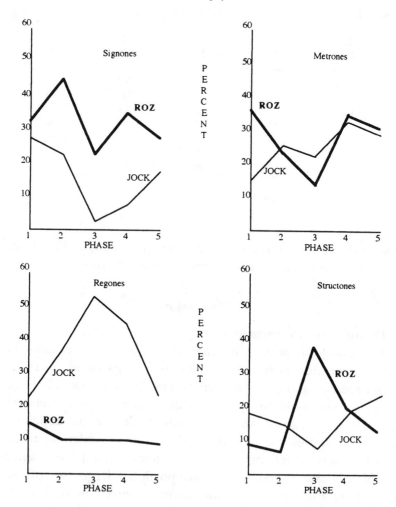

states (Signones) and in making evaluative statements (Metrones). She produced relatively few informational statements (Structones) except in response to questions or reporting some observation about the environment. Once she took over the rowing (Phase #2), however, self-descriptive content (Signones) increased, reflecting her growing apprehensiveness. At the peak of the crisis in Phase 3 she produced many requests for information (Regones), to learn quickly how better to control her environment. However, when the crisis had passed, Phase #5, a delayed emotional discharge occurred in the form of increased use of Signones and Metrones. Jock's behavior, in contrast, is characterized by the high rate of requests, demands, and prohibitions (Regones). His high output of Regones, started in Phase #1, continued to rise when Roz took over the oars, Phase #2, and reached its peak in the crisis of Phase #3. The authors summarize these inferences in the following manner:

> Yet, even after the emergency had passed, he persisted in telling Roz what to do and attempted to re-create the superior-subordinate relation that existed prior to the crisis. In this situation Regones and Metrones apparently served two purposes for Jock. At certain points they functioned principally to enhance his ego, and at other times their objective was to control the environment and thus allay his anxiety. . . . A first gross generalization about this young couple, then, might be that the wife was much more explicitly emotive than the husband whereas he tended to be the more active of the two in structuring and directing interpersonal events. Whether these patterns are due to sex differences, age differences, or even the particular selection of episodes remains an open question. (pp. 276–279)

3. The Effects of Recording

A major concern of Soskin and John was how well the subjects would habituate to continuous recording of their conversations, and how this constant monitoring would influence their linguistic performance. They state that both subjects reported afterward that they were aware of such influence at some times and not at others, and that self-consciousness diminished with the passage of time. It is the authors' conclusion that

> self-consciousness seems to vary inversely with the degree of one's involvement with his [/her] environment. We have all managed at some time to forget completely, for example, the visible rip in the front of our garment once we become engrossed in conversation, and as wearers of eyeglasses or hearing aids or dental bridges will attest, one comes to terms rather quickly with a new and ever-present appurtenance. (p. 234)

4. Implications

Soskin and John point out an interesting and serendipitous aspect of their results: only 25 percent of the content categories uttered by Roz and Jock were of the information-giving variety, that is, Structones. However, 66 percent of the content categories used were Regones, Signones, and Metrones. From this lead, the authors suggest that another useful way to look at content is whether it is *informational* or *relational*; and whether relational content is directive or inductive. Directive content specifies behavior that will cause a desired relation. Inductive content, in contrast, merely provides information that will induce the interlocutor to respond with the desired behavior. The *informational-relational* and directive-inductive dichotomies can provide a taxonomy of content categories as follows:

Informational Content:
  Structone (objective report)
Relational Content:
  Directive: Regone (persuasion)
  Inductive: Signone (subjective report), Metrone (judgment)
Quasi- Relational Content:
  Inductive: Expressive (exclamation), Excogitive (thinking aloud)

Although Expressive and Excogitive contents are primarily of intrapersonal talk, if they are heard, they tend to have an inductive effect. Since these contents will sometimes be relational in effect, they are labeled *quasi-relational.*

Soskin and John doubt that the high percentage of relational content used by Roz and Jock is typical of the daily conversations of most married couples. This finding does, though, suggest a number of hypotheses about the nature of relational content: relational content may be more frequent between intimates than between strangers; relational content frequency may be positively correlated with the intensity of a relationship; relational content frequency may be influenced by maturity and may be a function of age; relational content may be more frequent in private conversations. The implication is that the ratio of Regones, Signones, and Metrones to other types of content in conversations may be an index of intimacy or social proximity. This implication can be formulated as: Intimacy = [persuasions + subjective reports + judgments] ÷ [exclamations + thinking aloud + objective reports].

8

Classic Experiments

A. General Comments

1. Statistical Inference

The lack of applying tests of statistical inference in the four classic studies abridged below does not stem from any anti-statistical inference principle. On the contrary, Sanford (1942, p. 811) states quite explicitly that his goal is to "... pave the way for a nomothetic science of language." The lack of tests of statistical inference stems from the fact that the techniques for statistical inference were not highly developed then. A check of a well respected and long popular text (Winer, 1962) on statistical inference, indicates only two references to content articles related to statistical inference at the time these classic studies were published, one in 1940 and another in 1942. Boder does refer to a "Sigma Difference" and Sanford refers to the binomial expansion and associated levels of significance, but neither author employs these tools to point to statistically significant differences in their data.

2. The Abridgment Format

A second general comment is about the format for the abridgments of the four classic research articles. At the time these articles were written, there existed no standard form of publication, as that provided in the *Publication Manual* of the American Psychological Association. For consistency in presenting the information in these four articles a standard format was developed. The research article format in the American Psychological Association Publication Manual, and a review of published articles focusing on semiotic psychology research were the bases for the construction of this standard format.

B. Newman and Mather (1938, 1939)

1. Introduction

Newman conducted his first studies in the area of semiotic psychology while he was at the Department of Anthropology at Yale University. His collaborator in these studies was Vera G. Mather, a psychiatrist at the New Haven Hospital. The following is an abridgment that synthesizes two articles and the references are, accordingly, either to Newman and Mather or Newman.

Newman places his research in the context of an area of study focusing on the affective, connotative, and poetic aspects of speech sign behavior. He points out that "... the official function of language is rational communication; ... [however] when language is employed in the more commonplace everyday situations, particularly in the form of speech, its official function may be dimmed to the point of extinction" (p. 177). To emphasize this point, Newman quotes from the work of Malinowski (1923, p. 177), who had observed that in the language of "primitive" people the function of the exchange of words is often to establish interpersonal solidarity rather than to transmit specific information. Newman reminds the reader that Malinowski had identified and labeled this phenomenon as *phatic communication*.

In specifying the context in which he was working, Newman emphasizes the function of language and paralanguage as an index of emotions and attitudes. He stresses the point that the function of speech signs as indices of emotions and attitudes is as important as the function of speech signs as indices of cognitive states. Also, although the importance of speech signs as indices of emotions and attitudes had been pointed out by several prominent scholars, this semiotic psychology aspect of language and paralanguage was essentially ignored.

> Affective implications have been recognized in many of the phenomena of speech, such as intonation, accent, timbre, speech, etc. . . . Yet, the dogma persists that the function of language is intellectual and collective. Although other functions can be demonstrated, they are regarded as of distinctly minor importance; or, even worse, they are felt to be illegitimate intrusions upon the essentially rational and impersonal business of language. (p. 178)

Newman looked to the language of psychiatric patients as fertile ground for semiotic psychology research. He was aware of the fact that psychiatrists, in their clinical practice, had discovered the importance of *how* speech signs were produced rather than *what* was produced. The primary goal of Newman's research project was the identification of the objective linguistic and paralinguistic behaviors that led to these intuitive responses. His goal was to provide operational definitions for speech signs, so that the study of semiotic psychology would be transformed from a clinical art to a social science. In his words:

> The speech of patients has always played a prominent part in forming clinical impressions. However, little attention has been paid to the exact alterations to voice and language that combine to build the characteristics commonly thought of as associated with certain psychiatric syndromes. General descriptive terms have been used such as 'monotonous,' 'dull,' 'lifeless,' 'vivid,' 'dramatic' and 'emphatic.' It is of interest to learn what gives this 'coloring' to speech and whether or not specific speech characteristics are consistently associated with certain syndromes. (p. 913)

2. Methods

Subjects. The research reported here ". . . was limited to a group of patients with affective disorders. In all the patients studied, retardation or acceleration, and depression, euphoria or irritability were clearly manifest" (p. 913).

Newman and Mather's research with two categories of patients is presented: patients with classical depression and patients with manic syndromes. The patients included in the group labelled "classical depression," are described as experiencing:

> Circumscribed illnesses characterized predominantly by sadness of mood and retardation. Some showed agitation, tension and self-accusatory ideas. Insomnia, anorexia and constipation were usual. Some had experienced similar illnesses previously with recovery. A smaller number had had episodes of euphoria and acceleration. (p. 917)

W. N. is an example of a typical patient with classical depression.

> A 30-year-old American survey engineer first suffered from a period of low spirits at the age of 27 years. For about five months he exhibited

> depressed mood, decreased motor activity, insomnia, anorexia, increased shyness and diminished sexual potency. During the following year he was irritable, sexually promiscuous, alcoholic in episodes, and unable to hold any steady employment . . . he remained continuously depressed, but with a gradual diminution in the severity of his symptoms. (p. 918)

The patients included in group labelled "manic syndromes," are described as a group which:

> Included those syndromes characterized predominantly by acceleration with euphoria or irritability. Many showed grandiose trends. The illnesses were circumscribed. Many of the patients had had previous similar attacks or had experienced depressive episodes. (p. 926)

F. R. is an example of a typical patient with a manic syndrome.

> A 61-year-old- business man was in low spirits with weeping spells for one month. Garrulousness, irritability, confusion and disorientation then appeared . . . He showed marked pressure of speech, flight of ideas with superficial associations and motor overactivity. He sang, whistled, danced and talked incessantly. He described his mood as happy. During the next two months these features gradually decreased in intensity. (p. 927)

Speech Samples. The authors report that the recordings of the patients' spontaneous speech were elicited by questions from the psychiatrist and through short reading selections, and that ". . . the speech of the patients was recorded with microphone and phonograph equipment on cellulose acetate discs" (p. 914).

Speech Variables. Following are the operational definitions of the speech variables that Newman and Mather investigated.

1. Articulatory movements: lax ↔ vigorous.
   Although one may receive a general impression of the character of articulatory movements throughout a person's speech, the pronunciation of the stop consonants t, d, k, g provides the clearest indication. These consonants are produced by a closure of the tongue against the palate, followed by a release. In the speech of some persons, however, the closure is only partial or loosely made, and the release is lax; d or t, for example, will sound like a single-

trilled r. In the speech of others, the closure is tight and the release is crisp and vigorous; here the d or t may be accompanied by a slight click (p. 914).

2. Pitch Range: wide ↔ narrow.
   In English the greatest changes of pitch are ordinarily found at the end of sentences: the pitch falls at the end of declarative statements and raises at the end of interrogations. But rises and falls that extend over a wide pitch range in the speech of one person will be flattened in the speech of another (p. 914).
3. Tempo: slow ↔ fast.
4. Pauses: prosodic/hesitating.
   Prosodic pauses are silences that occur between phrases. Hesitating pauses are silences that occur within phrases.
5. Resonance: oral/nasal.
   Nasality results when the voice resonates in the nasal passage and escapes, either partially or wholly, through the nose (p. 915).
6. Glottal Rasp: present/absent.
   Glottal rasp is "... produced by an incomplete closure of the glottis; the entire glottis is made to vibrate, with some vertical as well as lateral motion. When rasping occurs, speech has a 'throaty trill' quality to it" (p. 916).
7. Words of Degree: infrequent/frequent.
   Words of degree represent bipolar conceptual scales such as 'wonderful' and 'terrible.'
8. Response Latency: short/long.
9. Response Length: short/long.

3. Results and Discussion

According to Newman and Mather the goal of their study "... was to ascertain whether certain characteristics of language are associated with particular syndromes" (p. 938). These authors did, in fact, discover particular 'colorings' of the speech of psychiatric patients. Specifically, they observed that the language of patients with classical depression and those with manic syndrome differed consistently in terms of a cluster of several clearly defined speech variables.

First, the analysis of the speech of patient W. N., a typical patient with classical depression, indicated the following characteristics:

> Lax articulatory movements throughout all recordings; narrow pitch range widening slightly in successive recordings; glottal rasping at beginning of statements; nasal resonance only in the first recording; a rapid tempo in reading, slower and more varied tempo in spontaneous speech; slow tempo at beginning of response; pauses of hesitation; short statements, several being phrase responses; slow initiation of response, becoming more rapid in final recording; short responses, containing one statement in first recording, later consisting of two or three statements. (p. 922)

Second, the speech of F.R., the typical patient with a manic syndrome, showed the following:

> Vigorous articulatory movements, relaxing slightly in the last recording; a wide range of pitch, becoming somewhat narrower in successive recordings; sudden spurts of speech in first two recordings, absent in final recording; prosodic pauses frequent in first recording, later becoming less marked, with pauses of hesitation appearing in last recording; full oral resonance; weak volume and huskiness in first recording; concepts of extreme degree expressed only in first recording; statements made by long complete predications; quick initiation of response; responses long at first, becoming progressively shorter. (p. 932)

Third, their observations of the cluster of the speech variables in 40 patients are summarized in Table 8.1:

Speech Variables	Classical Depressions	Manic Syndromes
1. Articulatory movements	lax	vigorous
2. Pitch Range	wide	narrow
3. Tempo	slow	fast
4. Pauses	prosodic	hesitating
5. Resonance	oral	nasal
6. Glottal Rasp	present	absent
7. Words of Degree	infrequent	frequent
8. Response Latency	short	long
9. Response Length	short	long

Table 8.1

In conclusion Newman and Mather indicate that the results of their observations imply three considerations for future research. First, they suggest a more detailed study of pitch: "An undoubtedly valuable contribution to the understanding of speech would be an intensive study of pitch, preferably with the help of a pitch discriminating apparatus that could give more accurate data than the unaided ear" (p. 940).

Second, they suggest the expansion of research in the area of semiotic psychology to include the study of content:

> In the present study, which was limited to small samples of speech from a number of patients it was not possible to deal with types of content as affecting the formal characteristics of a patient's language; content seemed to be particularly important in determining changes in the speech of patients showing states of dissatisfaction, self-pity, and gloom. A study based on a fuller sampling of speech from individual patients could deal with the factor of content more effectively than was a possible in this investigation. (p. 940)

Finally, Newman and Mather suggest that analysis of recordings taken at intervals over a period of years and "studied in the light of a thoroughgoing investigation of the life course of the individual" (p. 940) would likely yield instructive data on the relationship between language and paralanguage on the one hand, and emotions and attitudes on the other.

C. Balken and Masserman (1939, 1940)

1. Introduction

In a study of the fantasies of neurotic and psychotic patients, Masserman and Balken (1939) had observed:

> Not only did the phantasies reveal many of the important unconscious psychodynamisms of the patient's neurosis, but also that the style, structure, and other formal characteristics of the productions were often directly indicative of the predominant features of the mental status of the subject investigated. (p. 75)

In a subsequent publication, Balken and Masserman (1940) report that their observation of an association between language and paralanguage, on the one hand, and affective mental states, on the other, was reinforced by previous theoretical and experimental publications. In terms of theory, they point to statements by Sapir and Freud:

> Sapir (1921) has pointed out that, despite the inadequacies and limitations of ordinary language for the communication of affect ('emotion, indeed, is proverbially inclined to speechlessness') an individual's language is in subtle ways peculiar to him[/her] and an unmistakable signature of his[/her] personality. . . . Psychoanalytic theory, concerned rather with the motivations than with what Sapir calls the 'outer layer' of language, has adopted a more dynamic formulation. Freud (1904) pointed out the meaning of slips of the tongue, and analysts have since learned to recognize the significance not only of the content but also of the forms of expression used by their patient. (p. 82)

In terms of experimental evidence, there was Piaget (1926) who ". . . from an ontogenetic standpoint, has demonstrated the relationship of the forms of language with the mental development of the individual" (p. 82); and Southard (1916) suggested investigation of the relationship between grammatical elements and personality. Southard specifically indicated :

> Delusional statements of psychotic patients be analyzed for person, number, and gender of nouns and for voice, tense, and mood of the verbs, since the results might indicate a significant relationship of these parts of speech with 'whether the patient is manifestly and subjectively in an active and dominant relation to his fellows, in a passive relation thereto or in a personal plight of difficulties with himself.' Southard thought also that the indicative mood might denote the 'phlegmatic' temperament, the imperative the 'choleric,' and the optative the 'sanguine'. (p. 82)

These authors then refer to Busemann (1925) who ". . . analyzed the verbal productions of individuals aged 5 to 18 for the proportion of 'qualitative' or descriptive as opposed to 'active' or dynamic expressions" and, who concluded "that low values of the 'Action Quotient' thus obtained were a significant index of the emotional stability of the individual" (p. 83).

Balken and Masserman conclude their review of the literature with an interesting and provocative quotation from an article in which Stern (1925) had reviewed Busemann's work:

> Busemann is right when he speaks of an 'active' and a 'qualitative' style: he gives the interesting proof that these 'style' differences depend very little upon the subject matter dealt with. The 'actionale' person will express himself in the description of a landscape in 'active' terms . . .

> whereas the individual with a qualitative style will dwell even in reports of travel upon the description of more quiet impressions. The active; style correlates more closely with motility and emotions, with lower objectivity, less concreteness, and less intellectuality. The qualitative style reflects the opposite traits. Evidently, we have here a distinction similar to that which differential psychology long ago designated as 'subjective' and 'objective' types. (p. 84)

These theoretical statements by Sapir, Freud, Piaget, and Southard, in addition to the experimental investigations of Busemann, provided very strong support for Balken and Masserman's earlier observation that a relationship exists between specific language behaviors and specific mental states. It was, therefore, the aim of their second study

> to present a more specific analysis of these and other formal aspects of the language of phantasy . . . such as (a) that conversion hysterics produced phantasies which were flip and . . . and frankly sexual, (b) that the phantasies of patients with marked anxiety were characterized by moving, dramatic situations and intense, comparatively clear-cut conflicts and (c) that in the productions of obsessive-compulsive patients there was a pervading uncertainty–a sort of fruitless, querulous indecision in which 'perhaps,' 'maybe' . . . or equivalent expressions are common. (p. 75)

In order to accomplish their goal, Balken and Masserman created four objective indices of language behavior which they believed expressed specific mental states: (1) The Verb-adjective quotient, for which "high values connote restless, forceful, dramatic action . . . , expressing libidinal tensions and anxiety . . . ;" (2) The Pro-con quotient for which "high values evidence smoothness of narration corresponding with superficial emotional equanimity in the subject . . . ;" (3) The Certainty-uncertainty quotient for which "high values indicate emotional or defensive positiveness of assertion;" and (4) The Qualification-certainty quotient for which "high values express obsessive hesitation, doubt and self criticism"(p. 79).

2. Methods

Subjects. First, fifty patients were administered ". . . a complete medical and psychiatric diagnostic study," and in addition, "each patient was also given a battery of psychological tests." Second, "fifteen patients of uniformly high intelligence (IQ

118–138) were then selected in groups of five so that each group fitted most closely the respective clinical characteristics of conversion-hysteria, anxiety state, and obsessive-compulsive neurosis" (p. 76).

Speech Samples. To obtain samples of language behavior Balken and Masserman presented their subjects with pictures that they had obtained from the Harvard Psychological Clinic. These pictures depicted "situations to which a wide variety of phantasies could readily be associated," and there were "ten neutral pictures" and "ten pictures for men only" (p. 345). By "for men only" the authors mean that these are pictures with which men in this culture would identify with more readily than women.

> Before being shown the pictures the subject was informed, in a manner best calculated to win his cooperation, that he was to be given an opportunity to display his 'literary ability' or his facility in 'imagination.' He was then given the cards in series and requested to tell a story about the people or the situation in the picture and to carry his narrative through to any conclusion he desired. . . . The test was generally given in two periods a day or more apart, ten pictures being used at each session. No limitations were placed on the length of the phantasies nor on the time taken to tell them, so that a single testing session could last from one to three hours, during which verbatim records of the phantasies were taken by the examiner. (p. 345)

Speech Variables. The most important language measures reported by Balken and Masserman in terms of reliability and validity, are the four "indices," which they derived from nine basic language features. The first two language features they employed in their derived indices are grammatical:

1. *Verbs*. Active, passive and intransitive verbs.
   Verbs in all forms, including infinitives and participles, were counted. Participles used without nouns and preceded by an article–*the* or *a*–or by the preposition *of* and auxiliary verb (e.g., *have, shall,* etc.) were not counted (p. 78).
2. *Adjectives*. Predicative, participial and attributive adjectives.
   The adjective count included participial adjectives preceded by the article *the* or *a* or by the preposition *of,* but nouns used as adjectives, adjectives used as nouns (e.g., *the wealthy*,

the idle), quantitative and ordinal numerals and "numeral pronouns" (*next*, *many*, and *several*) and the adjectives *certain*, *various*, and *different* were not counted (p. 78).

In addition, Balken and Masserman employed seven semantic features in their derived measures:

1. *Expressions of possibility.*
   Statements such as "this is possible," "conceivable," and "it stands a chance."
2. *Expressions of probability.*
   Statements such as "thinks likely," to be expected," and "appears to be."
3. *Expressions of certainty.*
   Statements such as "positive," "sure," "no question," and "inevitable."
4. *Expressions of impossibility.*
   Statements such as "incredible," "unimaginable," and "unthinkable."
5. *Expressions of improbability.*
   Statements such as "not likely," "I don't think," and "chances are against"
6. *Expressions of uncertainty.*
   Statements such as "afraid to say," "wonder whether," and "I don't know."
7. *Expressions of qualification.*
   Statements indicating ". . . limitation, modification or reservation concerning an assertion."

As indicated, on the basis of the two grammatical features and the seven semantic features, four derived indices—each hypothesized to indicate a significant mental state-were examined:

1. *The Verb-adjective quotient.*
   The Verb-adjective quotient, abbreviated as "V-Aq," was obtained by dividing the total number of verbs in the speech sample by the total number of adjectives.

2. *The Pro-con quotient.*
   The Pro-con quotient, abbreviated as "P-Cq," was obtained by dividing the total number of Expressions of Possibility, Probability and Certainty by the total number of Expressions of Impossibility, Improbability and Uncertainty.
3. *The Certainty-uncertainty quotient.*
   The Certainty-uncertainty quotient, abbreviated as "C-Uq," was obtained by dividing the total number of Expressions of Certainty by the total number of Expressions of Uncertainty.
4. *The Qualification-certainty quotient.*
   The Qualification-certainty quotient, abbreviated as "Q-Cq," was obtained by dividing the total number of Expressions of Qualification by the total number of Expressions of Certainty.

3. Results and Discussion

The results of analyzing the fantasy productions of patients representing three psychodynamic states: anxiety state, conversion hysteria and obsessive-compulsive reaction, in terms of the four language behavior indices: V-Aq, P-Cq, C-Uq and Q-Cq are summarized in Table 8.2. This table indicates that patients who exhibited anxiety states had the largest V-Aq quotients and patients exhibiting conversion hysteria the lowest. Patients exhibiting conversion hysteria had the largest P-Cq and C-Uq quotients and patients exhibiting anxiety state the lowest. Finally, obsessive compulsive patients had the largest Q-Cq quotient and patients exhibiting conversion hysteria the lowest.

As Balken and Masserman had predicted, patients in each of the three psychodynamic state groups had characteristic narrative styles. However, along with these very supportive results,

	V-Aq	P-Cq	C-Uq	Q-Cq
Conversion Hysteria	1.4	6.7	3.5	2.0
Anxiety State	3.1	4.1	1.8	5.0
Obsessive-Compulsive	2.2	2.4	0.7	8.2

Table 8.2

Balken and Masserman caution that there is not a simple and direct one-to-one relationship between emotions or attitudes and speech sign behavior.

> It must be remembered . . . that other concurrent mental reactions were not excluded by our criteria; thus, in a separate series of psychoses studied by the same methods, a case of paranoia with marked homosexual anxiety scored a higher verb-adjective quotient [6.3] than any anxiety state in the present series, whereas the phantasies of depressed patients with concurrent obsessive-compulsive trends showed many of the features of the latter neurosis. . . . [I]n view of the variability and multiplicity of intrapsychic dynamisms present in every patient . . . only in cases which exhibit dominant psychic reactions in relatively pure form can the phantasies have a 'diagnostic' value . . . (pp. 84–85).

With this caveat in mind, the results do indicate strong support for Balken and Masserman's original observation that was the impetus for their research: a narrative may reveal many of important unconscious psychodynamisms which can be identified by examining the "style, structure, and other formal characteristics" of the speaker's language behavior.

D. Boder (1940)

1. Introduction

Although published in 1940, Boder's research was completed in 1927, at which time it was presented to the University of Chicago for a Master of Arts degree in psychology. A flurry of interest in the "psychological significance of the forms of linguistic expression" and frequent requests for copies of his research, stimulated Boder to publish his research in journal form. Boder suggests that his readers, whom he identifies as students of "the psychology of language," also refer to "An Objective Psychology of Grammar" by Kantor (1936), monographs on the Rorschach test by Samuel Beck (no date) and studies on thematic apperception and finger painting by Dr. Eva R. Balken (no date).

Boder credits the research of Busemann (1925) as providing the impetus for his own investigation. Busemann had proposed an index of language usage, the Action Quotient, which he had derived by dividing the number of verbs by the number of adjectives. Busemann had concluded that

> the relative number of adjectives does not increase steadily with age, but that a rhythmical increase and decrease of the Action Quotient occurs, corresponding to rhythmical changes of emotional stability during childhood adolescence, and youth. (p. 311)

Apparently two aspects of Busemann's work captured Boder's research interest. First was Busemann's conclusion that a specific, direct relationship linked the Action Quotient to the emotional state of the speaker that was independent of the speaker's stage of language development. Second, was the extension of Busemann's claim indicating that the Action Quotient was also independent of the content of discourse:

> Stern (1925) writes: Busemann is right when he speaks of an 'active' and a 'qualitative' style; he gives the interesting proof that those 'style differences' *depend very little upon the subject matter dealt with.* The 'kinesthetic' person will express himself[/herself] even in the description of a landscape in 'active' terms . . . the individual with a qualitative style will dwell even in traveling reports upon the description of more quiet impressions. The *active* style coincides more closely with motility and emotionality, with lower objectivity, less concreteness and less intellectuality. The qualitative style reflects the opposite trait. We evidently have here a distinction similar to that which differential psychology long ago has designated as 'subjective' and 'objective' types. (pp. 312–313, emphases in original)

Boder surmised that the hypothesis underlying the statements by Busemann and Stern was ". . . that the use of the attributive adjective, especially when located before the noun, corresponds to a higher type of ideational and linguistic behavior than is usually required by other speech forms . . ." (p. 314). Boder further surmised that it was this hypothesis that led Busemann and Stern to the conclusion that the relative use of verbs and adjectives was independent of both the stage of language development of the speaker and the subject matter being discussed. It was this conclusion that provided Boder with the rationale for his research:

> If it is true that the use of the attributive adjective . . . corresponds to a higher type of ideational and linguistic behavior than is usually required by other speech forms, then the assumption that it may be

> more easily affected by factors usually considered influencing either mental or motor activity seems also justified. . . . Thus in the present study we were interested in determining whether there exist gross differences of adjective-verb ratios corresponding to differences in subject matter of various classes of writing, a fact apparently denied, at least to a certain extent, by Busemann and especially Stern. (pp. 315–316)

It should be noted that Boder did not consider the possibility that different subject matter may also be affected by factors usually considered influencing either mental or motor activity, and therefore, different subject matter, like different emotional states, may require a "higher type of ideational and linguistic behavior." In Stern's terminology, there may be subjective and objective types of subject matter. Viewed from this perspective, Boder's study can be viewed as a test of the hypothesis ". . . that the use of the attributive adjective, especially when located before the noun, corresponds to a higher type of ideational and linguistic behavior than is usually required by other speech forms. . . ." Specifically, if the hypothesis is correct, subject matter that expresses great mental effort or precision and little spontaneity should exhibit increased use of adjectives relative to verbs; whereas subject matter that expresses great spontaneity and little mental effort or precision should exhibit increased use of verbs relative to adjectives.

2. Methods

Language Sources. Boder sampled the language in the writing of plays, legal writing, fiction, and science. His intent was to sample categories of writing that represented four distinctly different purposes and contents, which he labeled "conversational" (the plays); "normative" (the legal statutes); "narrative" (the fiction); and, "descriptive" (the science). He obtained samples from 20 plays: "10 plays were taken from J. Moses' *Representative American Dramas*, the other ten were chosen from Quinn's *Contemporary American Plays*, or from B. Mantle's *Best Plays* (p. 318). Samples of legal writing were obtained from the Illinois Revised Statutes (1923) and from the U.S. Federal Codes (1926). The samples of fiction writing were obtained from 20 novels, 10 written by men and 10 by women. "The authors were recommended by the reference librarians of the Chicago Public

Library and of the library of the University of Chicago, as the most popular" (p. 321). There were also samples of science writing from Ph.D. and Master's theses, scientific textbooks, and the collections "Psychologies of 1925" and "The Nature of the World and of Man" (p. 322).

Language Samples. For fiction and science writing, samples consisted of 300 to 350 continuous words. For plays and legal writing, a sample consisted of 50 continuous verbs, which corresponded to approximately 200 to 250 words. Boder states that "In a few cases the desired length or number of specimens was not obtainable" (p. 319).

Language Variables. Following Busemann, Boder counted the frequency of adjectives and verbs the language samples, and he stated very specific rules for identifying words exhibiting these grammatical categories (p. 316).

For adjectives:

1. Only attributive adjectives were counted, i.e., only adjectives placed before the noun.
2. Nouns used as adjectives (*rubber* tire, *ginger* bread) were not counted.
3. Adjectives used as nouns (the *poor*, the *rich*) were not counted.
4. Quantitative and ordinal numerals and 'numeral pronouns' (*next*, *many* and *several*) were not counted, nor was the adjective *certain*, because of its indefiniteness.

For verbs:

5. Verbs in all forms, including infinitives and participles (except as described under point 6) were counted.
6. Participles used without nouns and preceded by an article (*the* or *a*) or by the preposition *of* were not counted.
7. No forms of *have* and *be* were counted, nor were *could*, *should* and *would*.

The Adjective-Verb Quotient. Boder's index of language behavior, the adjective-verb quotient, was derived by dividing the number of adjectives in a sample by the number of verbs in that sample. This quotient "designates the number of attributive adjectives *per hundred verbs* in a given text, e.g., an Adjective-verb quotient of 15 means that the number of adjectives in the text amount to 15% *of the number of verbs*" (p. 317). It should be noted that this is an inversion of the index used by Busemann. In Busemann's quotient the number of verbs was the numerator and the number of adjectives the denominator, whereas in Boder's quotient the reverse was the case. Boder says that he adopted this procedure "to obtain a measure which might, if Busemann is right, correlate positively with desirable traits" (p. 317).

3. Results and Discussion

Table 8.3 lists the Adjective-verb quotients obtained for the four types of text studied. This table shows that the Adjective-verb quotients do vary according to the style of the writing: Avq = 8.8 for the "conversational style" expressed in the plays; Avq = 20.0 for the "normative style" expressed in the legal statutes; Avq = 35.2 for the "narrative style" expressed in the fiction; and, Avq = 75.5 for the "descriptive style" expressed in the science. In Boder's words, "We see then that the number of adjectives per 100 verbs is least in drama, slightly more in legal statutes, increases markedly in fiction, and reaches its highest value in scientific writing" (pp. 124–125).

Table 8.3 indicates that the largest difference between Avqs, 64.3, occurred between conversational style as expressed in plays and the descriptive style as expressed in scientific writing.

	Plays	Statutes	Fiction	Science
Plays	<u>11.2</u>	8.8	24.0	64.3*
Statutes		<u>20.0</u>	15.5	55.5
Fiction			<u>35.2</u>	40.3
Science				<u>75.5</u>

Underline = The mean Adjective-verb quotient for the type of text indicated.
Plain print = The difference in the mean Adjective-verb quotients between the two types of text indicated.
*= The largest difference between two Adjective-verb quotients.

Table 8.3

Boder explains this most dramatic difference in his results as follows:

> In plays the personal pronoun is used quite frequently; and likewise frequent use is made of the proper name (Helen, Henry, etc.) which stands for the individual with all his [sic!] previously given characteristics; the use of the adjective in conjunction with the proper name (little Jimmy, old Joe, etc.) is, where style is concerned, a definite exception. In this respect it must be observed that [in] science, . . . there is a tendency to preserve the combined descriptive terminology such as 'positive protons,' 'negative electrons,' rather than to invent names that would designate the phenomenon in one conventional word. . . . [I]n our opinion these facts corroborate the conclusion suggested by the low Avq in plays: everyday language, contrary to scientific style, tends to reduce significantly the number of adjectives used, probably in the interest of both the speaker and the hearer. (p. 327)

Table 8.3 also indicates that the second largest difference between Avqs, 55.5, occurred between normative style as expressed in legal statutes and the descriptive style as expressed in scientific writing. Boder explains that this difference may result from the fact that

> Statutes deal mainly with acts of human beings; they restrict to a certain extent the freedom of action and intend to prescribe as precisely as possible certain ways of conduct of citizens and of governmental agents. . . . On the other hand, scientific writings seem to deal with the mutual relations of men, animals, and things as consequences of their more or less constant qualities. . . . It seems that the precision achieved by legal statutes mainly through the verb is accomplished in science to a large extent through the adjective. (pp. 327–328).

Boder summarizes his results as follows: (1) The low Avq in the plays ". . . suggests that the necessity of fast and spontaneous verbal reactions during the dialogue reduces the number of adjectives" (p. 329); (2) The low Avq of legal statutes compared with the high Avq in scientific monographs suggests

> (a) law deals mainly with human beings and their acts while science deals with objects and their relatively permanent properties; (b) the act is more easily identified and defined than the quality; (c) the scientific monograph in its modern form is from an historical point of view the newest type of writing and is designated for a trained reader and thinker. (p. 329)

As indicated in the Introduction to this section, Boder's study can be seen as a test of the hypothesis that there exist subjective and objective types of subject matter. In addition, subject matter that expresses great mental effort or precision and little spontaneity should exhibit increased use of adjectives relative to verbs; whereas subject matter that expresses great spontaneity and little mental effort or precision should exhibit increased use of verbs relative to adjectives. The large difference Avq that Boder found between conversational style as expressed in plays and the descriptive style as expressed in scientific writing lends credence to this hypothesis.

E. Sanford (1942b)

1. Introduction

Sanford describes his study as "... an exploration of linguistic individuality" which "... presents and evaluates a method for dealing with linguistic style" (p. 169). Speaking style is the result of an individual's selection of the various aspects of language and paralanguage that together create a congruent pattern or *Gestalt*. Sanford cautions that by focusing on any one linguistic or paralinguistic feature–as he is doing in this study–it is possible to lose sight of the overall pattern.

> The style that survives statistical analysis seems less rich and less complete than the style we intuitively perceive in talking with [the individual]. But an analytical and quantitative picture of the individual's manner of speaking, though it may lack the subtler shades of the original, will have a certain utility. It will enable us to apply . . . science to the phenomena of style. (p. 169)

Sanford views his project as part of the general area of research that attempts "to measure the individual's expressive behavior" (p. 170), and that it derives its theoretical and methodological foundations from the work on expressive behavior by Allport and Vernon (1933). In a separate publication, Sanford (1942a) reviewed the literature in the specific area of expressive behavior he investigated and which he labeled "Speech and Personality." In the article being abridged here, he states that his review of the literature indicated that: "(1) linguistic behavior is intimately tied up with personal adjustment and (2) the individual's verbal behavior may be treated profitably by analytical devices" (p. 170).

The study reported here is the result of Sanford's intensive, and extremely detailed investigation of the linguistic and paralinguistic behavior of two Harvard students, identified as "Merritt" and "Chatwell." Sanford states that his goal is to produce an objective picture of the linguistic traits characterizing Merritt and Chatwell (p. 169).

> At the level of impression, Merritt and Chatwell have unique manners of speaking that is rooted deep in their personalities. Such impressions of style are rich and convincing, but they are always somewhat unsatisfactory, for all you can do with an impression is to have it. The present study, proceeding by analysis and quantification, describing style in terms that can be communicated, tested, built upon, seeks to transform impressions into knowledge. (p. 169)

2. Methods

Subjects. The two subjects of this study, Chatwell and Merritt, were both college sophomores, twenty years of age, with approximately the same grade point average, and both verbally productive.

Context. The experimental session was conducted in an ordinary room of informal appearance. In a preliminary warm-up period, the experimenter ". . . attempted to make the subject feel at home" (p. 171). All instructions to the subjects were given orally, and the responses of the subjects were recorded by a concealed microphone.

Speech Samples. The subjects were asked to respond orally to five different types of stimuli: 1) *Paintings*: "the subject was presented with prints of five paintings by well-known artists and asked to comment freely, giving his own impressions and reaction;" 2) *Scenes*: "each subject described a designated scene, familiar to both subjects;" 3) *3-Words*: "each subject was given a stimulus card containing a 'text-island' of three words and asked to create narrative around these words or around the ideas the words suggested;" 4) *10-Words*: the subjects were given similar instructions for "text-islands of ten words;" and 5) *Recalled Stories*: ". . . the subjects were required to reconstruct a semi-narrative piece of writing which they had read just before the previous meeting with the experimenter" (p. 171).

Sanford reports that speech samples were also obtained at a second experimental session, which occurred a week later, and

Stimulus	Chatwell	Merritt
1) Paintings	478	627
2) Scenes	657	563
3) 3-Words	2024	1231
4) 10-Words	1442	1315
5) Recalled Stories	352	588
6) Writing	1660	1296
Total	6613	5620

Table 8.4

during which "the procedure was identical except that different but 'equivalent' stimuli were used" (p. 171).

Writing Samples. In addition to the samples of spoken responses, Sanford bases his results on samples of language that he obtained from "autobiographies which Chatwell and Merritt had written in connection with another investigation" (p. 171).

Table 8.4 indicates the number of words obtained from each category of sample: 1) *Paintings;* 2) *Scenes;* 3) *3-Words;* 4) *10-Words;* 5) *Recalled Stories;* and 6) *Writing.*

Speech Variables. Sanford's first step in analyzing the language style of Chatwell and Merritt was to transcribe verbatim, in type-written form, the phonograph records of the speech samples. He then coded the speech and written samples for different language variables, which he groups in three categories: (1) "mechanical," (2) "psycho-grammatical," and (3) "composite categories."

An example of Sanford's "mechanical" language variables relates to what he refers to as "hesitating sounds," which in more current terminology are referred to as "filled pauses." Sanford coded 9 language variables in relation to filled pauses: 1) at the beginning of a clause; 2) two occurrences in a clause; 3) more than 2 within a clause; 4) within a verb phrase; 5) within a prepositional phrase; 6) between modifier and modified; 7) between phrases; 8) with repetitions; and 9) the total number of hesitating sounds.

One example of a "psycho-grammatical" language variable is in relation to "sentences." Sanford coded 6 sentence variables:

1) sentence length; 2) number of clauses in sentence; 3) simple sentence; 4) compound sentence; 5) complex sentence; and 6) compound-complex sentence.

"Composite categories" consists of derived variables: indices, ratios, groupings and totals. One example of Sanford's "composite categories," relates to the relative use of verbs and adjectives. Referring to the verb-adjective ratios devised by Busemann (1925) and Boder (1940) as "relatively blunt instruments for treating the active-qualitative dimensions of the person's speech" (p. 181), Sanford devised four different ratios reflecting the relative use of verbs and adjectives: 1) the "Gross Verb-Adjective ratio," which is essentially the same as Busemann's "Action Quotient" and Boder's "Adjective-Verb Quotient;" 2) the "Verb-Descriptive Adjective ratio," in which only descriptive adjectives are included; 3) the "Action verb-Descriptive Adjective ratio," in which the ". . . most static verbs and the least qualitative adjectives are left out"; and 4) the "Action-Description ratio," which includes ". . . the more verb-like and the more adjective-like participles" (p. 181).

In this manner Sanford identified and coded 7,488 different language variables. Sanford provides only a very brief list of these variables, and this list is, in Sanford's words ". . . bare of detail, with only brief explanatory comments or illustrations accompanying those most likely to be unfamiliar to the reader" (p. 173). However, Sanford is the first scientist reporting on semiotic psychology research to be concerned with the issue of reliability and states:

> The classification of linguistic constructions involves relatively complex judgments. Hence there is room both for intra- and inter-individual disagreement concerning the proper classification of many of the usages. Before we can trust completely the results of any linguistic analysis, the categories employed should be proven reliable. (p. 182)

Consistent with this concern for reliability of coding, he refers the reader to operational definitions for his 7,488 language variables:

> Since the reliable application of these categories requires that each be carefully defined with an eye to exceptions and special cases, the original list of rubrics is of too ponderous proportions to include here. For

> the reader who is interested in a more detailed account of the categories, the material is available. (in Sanford, 1941, p. 173)

Also consistent with his concern for reliability of coding, Sanford devised a method of evaluating the reliability of the 7,488 language variables he had coded. Sanford used a "test-retest" form of reliability in that he examined his ability to agree with himself after a period of one year had elapsed from the time he had performed the original coding (p. 182). Sanford re-coded 160 clauses of each subject and reports that, by carefully studying the operational definitions of the language variables, he was ". . . able to secure approximately the same results as obtained the previous year" and that the results of his reliability check

> may be taken as evidence that it is possible to secure good intra-individual reliability in the use of linguistic categories. Also they suggest that if the definition of the categories is sufficiently clear and explicit, inter-individual reliability of the same magnitude may be achieved. (p. 182)

In terms of current use of computer technology, it is interesting to quote at length how Sanford dealt with raw data that consisted of so many language variables.

> The analysis employed the punch-card method of scoring and tabulating. The first step was to divide each sample of speech into clausal units and to assign a separate Hollerith card to each clause. Each of the analytical rubrics employed was assigned to one of the many squares on the card. Then each clause was inspected for the linguistic constructions appearing therein. When a given construction, e.g., a possessive pronoun or an adverb of degree, appeared in the clause under analysis, the appropriate square was punched on the card representing that clause. Thus, by inspecting the card for, say, the first clause in Chatwell's [Recalled] Story, we can see that the clause is eight words in length, independent, contains one abstract noun, two limiting adjectives, a personal pronoun, etc. By machine computation it is possible to determine how many of the clauses in any sample of speech contain any given linguistic usage. (p. 173)

3. Results

As was indicated above, Sanford obtained eight speech samples by having the subjects respond twice, in separate sessions, to four stimuli: Paintings, Scenes, 3-Words, and, 10-Words. In addition, he obtained 1 sample from the speech in "Retold Stories," and two samples from written autobiographies. The 7,488 language variables were coded in each of these 11 samples, and were the basis of the *differentiation score*, which was ". . . the basic device for representing the differences between Chatwell and Merritt" (p. 183). Table 8.5 indicates how one such differentiation score was obtained. The numbers in this table represent the percentage of clauses that contained the language variable "cognitive verbs." The asterisk indicates that for one of the subjects, cognitive verbs occurred in a greater percentage of the clauses than for the other subject. The sum of the asterisks is the differentiation score. In this case, Chatwell's percentage of cognitive verbs is greater for two of the stimulus conditions, whereas Merritt's percentage is greater in eight. The differentiation score is, therefore, 2-8.

Having reliably coded 7,488 language variables and deriving a differentiation score for each, Sanford faced the task of synthesizing this huge number of ". . . discrete, uncoupled facts . . . into flesh-and-blood pictures of linguistic individuality" (p. 185).

Stimulus	Chatwell	Merritt
1) Paintings		
Session 1	6.8	*19.0
Session 2	8.3	*19.5
2) Scenes		
Session 1	*5.0	0.0
Session 2	0.0	0.0
3) 3-Words		
Session 1	*13.5	7.2
Session 2	6.0	*14.6
4) 10-Words		
Session 1	12.0	*24.0
Session 2	8.3	*10.0
5) Recalled Stories	4.5	*12.3
6) Writing		
Session 1	6.0	*8.0
Session 2	10.0	*20.0
Differentiation Score	2	8

Table 8.5

To accomplish this synthesis, he compiled two lists: one indicating all the linguistic variables, which according to the differentiation score, Chatwell's percentage per clause was greater than Merritt's; the other indicated all the linguistic variables, which according to the differentiation score, Merritt's percentage per clause was greater than Chatwell's (p. 186). Then, Sanford performed what might be labeled a "subjective factor analysis." In Sanford's own words: "The experimenter inspected each list, emerging with a group of linguistic traits for Chatwell and another for Merritt" (p. 186).

The major linguistic trait that emerged from Sanford's inspection of Merritt's list was "Complexity of Response." By inspection, Sanford recognized 13 discrete linguistic variables for which a) Merritt's differentiation score was greater than Chatwell's; and, more significantly in terms of the "subjective factor analysis," b) all 13 of these linguistic variables appeared to Sanford to "cohere meaningfully in the trait of complexity" (p. 186). Table 8.6 indicates the 13 discrete variables that Sanford grouped into the linguistic trait that he labeled "Complexity of Response."

On the bases of the differentiation scores for these 13 discrete variables, Sanford provides the following verbal description of Merritt's speaking style in relation to the linguistic trait he labeled "Complexity of Response:"

	Merritt	Chatwell
1. High index of subordination	*10	0
2. Many complex sentences	*8	3
3. Many compound-complex sentences	*9	2
4. High index of complexity	*10	0
5. Many second-order clauses	*10	1
6. Many third-order clauses	*10	1
7. Many fourth-order clauses	*7	2
8. Many clauses per sentence	*8	0
9. Long sentences	*9	1
10. Many relational clauses	*10	1
11. High relational-descriptive ratio	*8	2
12. Many parenthetical clauses	*8	2
13. Many parenthetical formulas	*8	2

Table 8.6

> Speaking, for Merritt, is a highly involved affair. Each sentence contains many clauses, and these clauses are tied intricately to one another.... The task of getting from one end of a sentence to the other involves many detours into subordination, many interpolations. His subordinate clauses are rarely the relatively simple descriptive clauses of 'where,' 'when,' and 'who,' but tend to run to the more elaborate relations of cause, consequence, and concession.... The complexity of his discourse is increased by his practice of including one clause parenthetically within another and by his use of the habitual parenthetical formulas such as 'so to speak,' or 'as I said.' This intricacy of response is probably the outstanding characteristic of his linguistic behavior. (p. 186)

In a similar factor-analytic like manner, Sanford identified a total of eight linguistic traits that expressed Merritt's overall speaking style: 1) Complexity of Response; 2) Perseveration; 3) Thoroughness of Response; 4) Lack of Coordination; 5) Static Nature of Rashness; 6) Clear Definition; 7) Cautiousness of Response; and, 8) Stimulus-bound Nature of Response. Then Sanford summarizes Merritt's overall speaking style as

> complex, complete, uncoordinated, cautious, perseverative, deferent, and stimulus-bound.... [W]e might conceive of his whole style as defensive and deferent.... Most of his verbal behavior seems to reflect a desire to avoid blame or disapproval. (p. 190)

Sanford identified the major linguistic trait that emerged from Chatwell's responses as "Color and Variety of Response." The ten discrete linguistic variables that appeared to Sanford to cohere meaningfully in a trait of "Color and Variety of Response" are listed in Table 8.7.

	Chatwell	Merritt
1. Many "rare" words	*10	1
2. High type-token ratio	*8	2
3. Many stylistic devices	*9	0
4. Many dead metaphors	*7	2
5. Frequent inversion of order	*7	1
6. Frequent slang expressions	*9	0
7. Many "impressive" adjectives	*9	2
8. Many contractions	*6	2
9. Many adverbs of manner	*5	2
10. Little repetition of content	*2	8

Table 8.7

On the basis of the differentiation scores for these 10 discrete variables, Sanford provides the following verbal description of Chatwell's speaking style in relation to the linguistic trait "Color and Variety of Response:"

> There is nothing jejune or conventional about Chatwell's speech. . . . His varied vocabulary, his use of 'impressive' adjectives, and his frequent slang expressions constitute the core of this tendency. The various stylistic devices, particularly the inversion of order (e.g., 'came June'), lend color and picturesqueness and the adverbs of manner add a note of liveliness. The frequency of contractions show his speech to be informal, and the rare repetition of content point to the absence of monotony. (p. 191)

Sanford then identifies a total of 14 linguistic traits that express Chatwell's unique speaking style: 1) Color and Variety of Response; 2) Emphasis and Intensity; 3) Directness of Response 4) Active Quality of Response; 5) Progressive Nature of Response; 6) Coordination of Response; 7) Characterization or Evaluation; 8) Inclusiveness and Lack of Reference; 9) Implicitness; 10) Connectedness of Discourse; 11) Confidence; 12) Autonomy in the Stimulus Situation; 13) Definiteness; and, 14) Enumeration. Then, percentage per clause, Sanford summarizes Chatwell's overall speaking style as

> colorful, varied, emphatic, direct, active, progressing always in a forward direction. His responses are well coordinated, closely interconnected, more evaluative than definitive, and somewhat enumerative. He covers extensive areas, verbally, and is disinclined to consider details or precision of reference. His speech is confident, definite, independent. In general he appears to use speech not so much to describe the external world and relations as to express his own individuality and to impress the auditor. (p. 197)

4. Discussion

By means of grouping 7,488 different language variables into 22 linguistic traits, Sanford was able to specify the overall speaking styles of observably different individuals. It seems apparent that the importance of his method is its success ". . . in revealing individual differences and giving pictures of style which, at the level of impression, have a decided ring of validity" (p. 197).

In evaluating his results, Sanford stresses that there are two obvious flaws in his research. First "the absence of group norms," by which he recognizes the fact that some of the deviations he identifies between the two speakers by means of his difference score may, in fact, be well within the bounds of normal deviations for these linguistic variables found in a large group of similar speakers. And second, the ". . . arbitrariness in the interpretation and grouping of some of the variables," by which he recognizes the weakness of the subjective factor analysis that he employed. However, Sanford was of the opinion that ". . . these difficulties can be ironed out in further research." In this vein, Sanford's intention to "iron out" these limitations of his methods in future research, provided the rationale for his use of the laborious Hollerith punch-card method described above:

> The punch-card method of analysis was employed with an eye to the eventual investigation of intra-individual patterns of response. It will be possible to determine, for example, whether Chatwell tends to use favorable modifiers in close conjunction with personal pronouns. Also, if interest is centered in the general psychology of grammar, it will be possible to determine what constructions occur in conjunction with what constructions and in what situation. We may eventually get to know the psychology of parts of speech by knowing what linguistic company they keep. (p. 173)

In other words, Sanford's long-term goal was to develop a research paradigm that would be the social science foundation of semiotic psychology.

Conclusion

The 1960s

In 1962, Thomas Sebeok organized the "Interdisciplinary Conference on Paralanguage and Kinesics" at the University of Indiana. The results of this conference were published in book form as *Approaches to Semiotics* (Sebeok et al.,1964). The content of this conference and the resulting book were indices, in one area of academia, of the 1960s' interdisciplinary mindset. It was in this atmosphere that conceptual formulations and research paradigms were integrated into the academic discipline described in this book. This is the context in which to understand Gallois' description of this book in her Foreword:

> *Semiotic Psychology* explores a body of psychological research, from the 1930s, 1940s, and 1950s, that focuses on naturally occurring language and its meanings. It provides an understanding of the theoretical and methodological backdrop of a body of research, undertaken at a time when social and clinical psychology were still strongly linked to psychophysics on the one hand and to psychoanalysis on the other.

It is the occurrence in one paragraph of: *naturally occurring language*, *meaning*, *social psychology*, *clinical psychology*, *psychophysics* and *psychoanalysis* that is the expression of the interdisciplinary *Zeitgeist* brought to bear on the study of speech as an index of emotions and attitudes. An examination of current literature will not find a similar juxtaposition of these words and phrases contiguously in one chapter or article, let alone one paragraph.

The preceding pages have explored the fundamental assumptions and research methods that, taken together, point to the academic discipline that emerged for the study of speech as index of attitude and emotion that the author has labeled *Semiotic Psychology*. Each academic discipline is delineated by a core concept, a research paradigm, and a central purpose. For Semiotic Psychology these are attitude, content analysis, and consciousness raising, respectively.

Core Concept: Attitude

An attitude is a relatively permanent mental set to respond in a positive or negative manner to a particular stimulus. The three socially critical characteristics of an attitude are (1) it is learned, (2) the stimulus that elicits the mental set does not have to be tangibly present for the mental set to be called forth, and, (3) it prepares a person to perform a particular behavior.

An attitude is the 'pro' or 'con' aspect of a particular value. The expression of an attitude is the extensional way we know that individuals hold a particular value; they approve or disapprove of certain political beliefs, they like or dislike certain religious ceremonies, they approach or avoid certain people.

The most important function of socialization is to teach children the attitudes that express the core values of the culture in which they live. Attitudes expressing core values are ready-made answers to socially significant questions. These ready-made answers are supplied by parents, friends, and teachers, and depend less on individual experience and more on accepting the viewpoints of significant others in the social environment. The primary conditioning factor in the learning of an attitude is social approval. Children learn the attitudes of significant others because they want their love and affection. The reason, when as adults we find it so difficult to raise our consciousness about certain unpleasant or disconcerting attitudes, is that these attitudes have been taught to us by people we admire and love.

Research Paradigm: Content Analysis

Content analysis, in general, is the description of messages by objective methods that are independent of the senders or receivers of these messages. Content analysis performed by semiotic psychologists, specifically, focuses on speech messages. These speech messages consist of signs that are either language or paralanguage. "Language signs" are analyzed in terms of phonetics, phonemics, morphemics, syntax, and semantics. These are structural levels of analysis that describe how the words of a language are produced and put together to make meaningful sentences. "Paralanguage Signs" are those non-language vocal gestures which may occur either simultaneously with or between words.

The chapters in this book on speech signs provide an understanding of the specific units of analysis that will be encountered in research that focuses on speech sign behavior. One or more of the language or paralanguage units described in these chapters will be found in any semiotic psychology study, regardless of the academic discipline of the author.

Either by language or paralanguage, our speech behavior indicates our thoughts about the here-and-now. This dimension of speech sign behavior is referred to as the principle of "immanent reference." The importance of this principle is that no matter what else you are talking about, or think you are talking about, you are always talking about the context in which your talking is taking place. The context includes your own physical and mental state, your attitudes toward the person to whom you are talking, and your attitudes toward the physical environment in which the talking is taking place.

Central Purpose: Consciousness Raising

The key implication of the principle of immanent reference is that we should always be prepared to ask to what extent and in what way the behavior of people talking to us is an index of their attitude/emotion towards us, and, to what extent is the way we talk to others an index of our attitude/emotion towards them. Focusing on speech signs as the behavioral manifestations of particular attitudes or emotions is the first step in consciousness raising. The second step is to verbalize the content of the attitude. In other words, consciousness is the ability to put into words the attitudes or emotions associated with particular speech signs. The greater the ability to verbalize the content of the attitude, the greater the consciousness. At the other extreme, if persons are unable to give a verbal account of the attitude or emotion associated with their behavior, they are said to be 'unconscious' of that behavior.

Speech signs provide an objective means for identifying the everyday expression of values and ideology, because values and ideology represent clusters of attitudes or emotions. It follows that the identification of particular attitudes and emotions provides a basis for identifying values and ideology. The implication of this triadic relationship between speech signs, attitudes/emotions, and values/ideology is that we can become conscious of speech signs that express attitudes/emotions that are not an accurate index of our own values/ideology. Consciousness raising provides the foundation to choose to send or receive messages that reflect our world views-the central purpose of *Semiotic Psychology* is to provide this choice.

Notes

Introduction

1 The model for this definition is Sebeok's definition of zoosemiotics: "The term *zoosemiotics* was launched in 1963 and initially proposed as a name for the discipline, within which the science of signs intersects with ethology, devoted to the scientific study of signaling behavior in and across animal species (1985, p. 294).

Chapter 2

1 Permission to use this cartoon has been granted by Mr. Borgman and King Features Syndicate.

2 This section benefited from reading Bugelski (1960, p. 410); Hayakawa (1978, pp. 176–80, Hollander (1976, pp. 155, 437), and, Klineberg (1954, pp. 511, 525–26, 512–19).

3 This section benefited from reading Allport (1961, pp. 414–18, 444–45), and, Barnouw (1963, pp. 176–77, 192–93).

4 This section benefited from reading Allport (1981, pp. 416–18, 444–45), and, King and Ziegler (1975, pp. 30–38).

Chapter 3

1 This section benefited from reading Allport (1961, pp. 181–86), Hollander (1976 pp. 214–15), and, Klineberg (1954, pp. 363–73).

2 Hall is referring to George L. Trager, the anthropological linguist, who worked with Hall at the Foreign Service Institute in Washington, D.C.

Chapter 4

1 <oxen> would be pronounced /aksɨn/ for most speakers of American English, however, in Eastern New England and in British English it is pronounced /ɔksɨn/. The /ɔ/ being pronounced like the vowel in <caught>.

2 This is only one part of the linguistic description of the plural affix of nouns in English. For a more detailed analysis see Gleason (1961, pp. 91–104).

Chapter 5

1 An extensive review of the early literature in this area can be found in Hymes (1964).

2 In this article Trager states: "As virtual co-authors must be mentioned Henry Lee Smith, Jr, Norman A. McQuown, and Ray L. Birdwhitstell" (p. 1). Also, Trager states that the linguist A. A. Hill coined the term paralanguage.

3 It is interesting to note that Trager identifies his work as "a first approximation" in spite of its obvious relation to the work of his mentor Sapir, and, in the entire article there is no reference to Sapir. In a similar vein, Pittenger et al. (1960) in a footnote on p. 194 of "The First Five Minutes," regarding the origins of paralinguistic studies in which they list the names of significant individuals, there is no reference to Sapir.

4 It is true that one can "talk through" the vocal characterizers listed, for example, talking while laughing. However, it is also true that such phenomena can occur by themselves, e.g., laughing.

Chapter 6

1 This abridgment and those appearing in chapters 8 and 9 have been organized into the format of a research article.

2 "In the spring of 1957, two of the three co-authors of this book were awarded a small grant by the National Institute of Mental Health. . . . for a research project officially entitled 'Linguistic-Kinesic Analysis of Schizophrenia.' . . . [In] 1959 a more extended grant from the National Institute of Mental Health was awarded for a new project officially entitled 'Linguistic-Psychiatric Analysis of Interview Samples'" (Pittenger et al., 1960, p. vii).

3 This transcription is modified somewhat for the present purposes. As to intonation, the pitch phonemes and the pitch phenomenon of "scoop" are not indicated, only the primary loudness phoneme is included. For ease of presentation, there are minor modifications in the numbering of turns, and the symbols used for the voice qualities and vocal segregates.

4 "Loudness" is more typically referred to as "stress" in linguistic parlance. I chose to use "loudness" to avoid any confusion in this context of discussing mental states.

5 From Pittenger, Hockett and Danehy's definition of "squeeze," and listening to the recording, it is apparent that the authors are referring to what is termed by other phoneticians "vocal fry," "laryngealization" "rasp" or "creak."

6 Diagonal lines (/ /) are a linguistic convention to indicate that the enclosed symbols represent phonemes.

References

Albee, G. W. (1981). The prevention of sexism. *Professional Psychology, 12* (1), 20–28.

Allport, G. W. (1942). The use of personal documents in psychological science. *Social Science Research Council Bulletin,* 49.

Allport, G.W. (1961). *Pattern and growth in personality.* New York: Holt, Rinehart and Winston.

Allport, G. W., & Vernon, P. E. (1933). *Studies in expressive movement.* New York: Macmillan.

Argyle, M. (1988). *Bodily communication.* (2nd ed.). London: Methuen.

Argyle, M., & Dean, J. (1965). Eye-contact, distance, and affiliation. *Sociometry, 28,* 289–304.

Balken, E. R., & Masserman, J. H. (1940). The language of phantasy: III. The language of the phantasies of patients with conversion hysteria anxiety state, and obsessive-compulsive neuroses. *Journal of Psychology, 10,* 75–86.

Ball, P., Gallois, C., & Callan, V. J. (1989). Language attitudes: A perspective from social psychology. In P. Collins & D. Blair (Eds.), *Australian English: The language of a new society* (pp. 89–102). St. Lucia: University of Queensland Press.

Barker, R. G., & Wright, H. F. (1955). *Midwest and Its children.* New York: Harper & Row.

Barker, R. G. (1960). Ecology and motivation. In M.R. Jones (Ed.), *Nebraska Symposium on Motivation* (pp. 1–49). Lincoln: University of Nebraska Press.

Barnouw, V. (1963). *Culture and personality.* Homewood: Dorsey Press.

Birdwhistell, R. L. (1952). *Introduction to kinesics: An annotation system for analysis of body motion and gesture.* Louisville, KY: University of Louisville Kentucky Press.

Birdwhistell, R. L. (1970). *Kinesics and context: Essays in body motion communication.* Philadelphia: University of Pennsylvania Press.

Boder, D. P. (1940). The adjective-verb quotient: A contribution to the psychology of language. *Psychological Record, 3,* 310–343.

Brown, R. (1958). *Words and things.* New York: Free Press.

Brown, R., & Gilman, A. (1960). The pronouns of power and solidarity. In T. A. Sebeok (Ed.), *Style in language* (pp. 253–256). Cambridge, MA: MIT Press,.

Bugelski, B. R. (1960). *An introduction to the principles of psychology.* New York: Rinehart & Co.

Burgoon, J. K., Buller, D. B., & Woodall, W. G. (1989). *Nonverbal communication.* New York: Harper & Row.

Busemann, A. (1925). *Die Sprache der Jugend als Ausdruck der Entwicklungsrhythmik.* Jena.

Chomsky, N. (1957). *Syntactic structures.* The Hague: Mouton.

Chomsky, N. (1965). *Aspects of the theory of syntax.* Cambridge, MA: MIT Press.

Cornforth, M. (1963). *The theory of knowledge.* New York: International Publishers.

Coupland, N., Coupland, J., & Giles, H. (1991). *Language, society, and the elderly.* Oxford: Blackwell.

Coupland, N., Coupland, J., Giles, H., & Henwood, K. (1988). Accommodating the elderly: Invoking and extending a theory. *Language in Society, 17,* 1–41.

Culler, J. (1976). *Saussure.* London: Fontana.

Davis, T. K. (1935). Sounds in language. *Journal of Nervous and Mental Disorders,88,* 491–500.

Eldred, S. H., & Price, D. B. (1958). A linguistic evaluation of feeling states in psychotherapy. *Psychiatry, 21,* 115–121.

Exline, R. V. (1972). Visual interaction: The glances of power and preferences. In J. Cole (Ed.), *Nebraska Symposium on Motivation,* Vol. 19 (pp. 163–206). Lincoln: University of Nebraska Press.

Fillmore, C. J. (1968). The case for case. In E. Bach & R.T. Harms (Eds.), *Universals in linguistic theory.* New York: Holt, Rinehart, and Winston.

Fiske, J. (1990). *Introduction of communication studies* (2nd ed.). New York: Routledge.

Freud, S. (1904). *Psychopathology of everyday life.* New York: Modern Library.

Fries, C. C. (1952). *The structure of English.* New York: Harcourt, Brace and Company.

Fromkin, V., & Rodman, R. (1988). *An introduction to language.* New York: Holt, Rinehart and Winston.

Gallois, C. (1994). Group membership, social rules, and power: A social psychological perspective on emotional communication. *Journal of Pragmatics* (Special Issue on Language and Involvement), *22,* 301–324.

Gallois C., & Markel, N. N. (1975). Turn taking: Social personality and conversational style. *Journal of Personality and Social Psychology, 31,* 1134–1140.

Gallois, C., Franklyn-Stokes, A., Giles, H., & Coupland, N. (1988). Communication accommodation in intercultural encounters. In Y. Y. Kim & W. B. Gudykunst (Eds.), *Theories in intercultural communication* (pp. 157–185). Newbury Park, CA: Sage.

Gardner, R. C., & Lambert, W. E. (1972). *Attitudes and motivation in second language learning.* Rowley, MA: Newbury House.

Giles, H. (1973). Accent mobility: A model and some data. *Anthropological Linguistics, 15,* 87–105.

Giles, H., & Powesland, P. F. (1975). *Speech style and social evaluation.* London: Academic Press.

Giles, H., & St. Clair, R. (Eds.). (1979). *Language and social psychology.* Oxford: Blackwell.

Giles, H., & Coupland, N. (1991). *Language: Contexts and consequences.* Milton Keynes: Open University Press.

Gill, M., Newman, R., & Redlich, F. C. (1956). *The initial interview in psychiatric practice.* New York: International Universities Press.

Gleason, H. A. (1961). *An introduction to descriptive linguistics.* New York: Holt, Rinehart and Winston.

Gottschalk, L. A. (1979). *The content analysis of verbal behavior.* New York: SP Medical & Scientific Books (Spectrum Publications).

Gottschalk, L. A., & Gleser, G. C. (1969). *The measurement of psychological states through the content analysis of verbal behavior.* Berkeley: University of California Press.

Gottschalk, L. A., Lolas, F., & Viney, L. L. (1986). *Content analysis of verbal behavior: significance in clinical medicine and psychiatry.* Berlin: Springer Verlag.

Gottschalk, L. A., Winget, C. N., & Gleser, G. C. (1969). *Manual of instructions for using the Gottschalk-Gleser content analysis scales: Anxiety, hostility, and social alienation–personal disorganization.* Berkeley: University of California Press.

Grice, H. P. (1975). Logic and conversation. In P. Cole & J. Morgan (Eds.), *Syntax and semantics, Vol. 3: Speech acts* (pp. 41–58). New York: Academic Press.

Guerin, B. (1994). *Analysing social behavior: Behavior analysis and the social sciences.* Reno, NV: Context Press.

Hall, C. S., & Lindzey, G. (1957). *Theories of personality.* New York: Wiley.

Hall, E. T. (1959). *The silent language.* New York: Doubleday & Co.

Halliday, M. A. K. (1978). *Language as social semiotic.* London: Edward Arnold.

Hargreaves, W. A. (1955). An investigation of time periods in spontaneous conversation. Unpublished master's thesis, University of Chicago.

Harper, R. G., Wiens, A. N., & Matarazzo, J. D. (1978). *Nonverbal communication: The state of the art.* New York: Wiley.

Harris, M. (1975). *Culture, people, nature: An introduction to general anthropology.* New York: Crowell.

Hayakawa, S. I. (1978). *Language in thought and action.* New York: Harcourt Brace Jovanovich.

Hodge, R., & Kress, G. (1988). *Social semiotics.* Cambridge: Polity Press.

Hollander, E. P. (1976). *Principles and methods of social psychology.* New York: Oxford University Press.

Holsti, O. R. (1968). Content analysis. In G. Lindzey & E. Aronson (Eds.), *The Handbook of social psychology.* Reading, MA: Addison-Wesley.

Hymes, D. (1961). Linguistic aspects of cross-cultural personality study. In B. Kaplan (Ed.), *Studying personality cross-culturally* (pp. 313–359). Elmsford, New York: Row, Peterson and Company.

Hymes, D. (1964). *Language in culture & society.* New York: Harper & Row.

Hymes, D. (1972). Models of the interaction of language and social life. In J. J. Gumperz & D. Hymes (Eds.), *Directions in sociolinguistics: The ethnography of communication* (pp. 35–71). New York: Holt, Rinehart, and Winston.

Jakobson, R. (1960). Linguistics and poetics. In T. A. Sebeok (Ed.), *Style in language* (pp. 350–77). Cambridge: MIT Press.

Jones, E. E., Kanouse, D. E., Kelley, H. H., Nisbett, R. E., Valins, S., & Weiner, B. (Eds.). (1972). *Attribution: Perceiving the causes of behavior.* Morristown, NJ: General Learning Press.

Kelley, H. H. (1972). Causal schemata and the attribution process. In E. E. Jones (Ed.), *Attribution: Perceiving the causes of behavior.* Morristown, NJ: General Learning Press.

Kendon, A. (1970). Movement coordination in social interaction: Some examples described. *Acta Psychologica, 32,* 100–125.

King, M., & Ziegler, M. (1975). *Research projects in social psychology.* Monterey, CA: Brooks Cole.

Klineberg, O. (1954). *Social psychology.* New York: Henry Holt & Co.

Knapp, M. L., & Hall, J. A. (1992). *Nonverbal communication in human interaction* (3rd ed.). Fort Worth: Harcourt Brace Jovanovich.

Kubie, L. S. (1958). The neurotic process as the focus of physiological and psychoanalytic research, *Journal of Mental Science, 104,* 518–536.

Labov, W. (1966). *The stratification of English in New York City.* Washington, DC: Center for Applied Linguistics.

Lambert, W. E. (1967). A social psychology of bilingualism. *Journal of Social Issues, 23,* 91–109.

Lambert, W. E., Gardner, R., Hodgson, R., & Fillenbaum, S. (1960). Evaluational reactions to spoken language. *Journal of Abnormal and Social Psychology, 60,* 44–51.

Lambert, W. E., Havelka, J., & Crosby, C. (1958). The influence of language acquisition contexts on bilingualism. *Journal of Abnormal and Social Psychology, 60,* 44–51.

Langacker, R. (1990). *Concept, image, and symbol: The cognitive basis of grammar.* Berlin and New York: Mouton.

Linton, R. (1945). *The cultural background of personality.* New York: Appleton-Century-Co.

Lomax, A., & Halifax, J. (1968). Folk song texts as cultural indicators. In A. Lomax, *Folk song style and culture* (pp. 274–299). Washington, DC: American Association for the Advancement of Science. (Publication No. 88).

Mahl, G. F., & Schulze, G. (1964). Psychological research in the extralinguistic area. In T. A. Sebeok, A. S. Hayes, & M. C. Bateson (Eds.) *Approaches to semiotics* (pp. 51–143). The Hague: Mouton.

Malinowski, B. (1923). The problem of meaning in primitive languages. In C. K. Ogden & I. A. Richards (Eds.), *The meaning of meaning* (pp. 296–336). New York: Harcourt, Brace, Jovanovich.

Markel, N., & Hamp, E. P. (1960). The connotative meaning of certain phoneme sequences. *Studies in Linguistics, 15,* 47–61.

Markel, N. (1965). The reliability of coding paralanguage: Pitch, loudness and tempo. *Journal of Verbal Learning and Verbal Behavior, 4* (4), 306–308.

Markel, N., Meisels, M., & Houck, J. E. (1964). Judging personality from voice quality. *Journal of Abnormal and Social Psychology, 69* (4), 458–463.

Markel, N., Phillis, J. A., Vargas, R., & Howard, K. (1972). Personality traits associated with voice types. *Journal of Psycholinguistic Research, 1*(3), 249–255.

Markel, N., Bein, M. F., & Phillis, J. A. (1973). The relationship between words and tone-of-voice. *Language and Speech. 16*(1), 15–21.

Masserman, J. H., & Balkan, E. R. (1939). Psychiatric and psychodynamic significance of phantasy. *Psychoanalytic Review, 26,* 343–379, 535–549.

McGuire, W. J. (1973). The yin and yang of progress in social psychology: Seven koan. *Journal of Personality and Social Psychology, 26,* 446–456.

McQuown, N. A. (1957). Linguistic transcription and specification of psychiatric interview material. *Psychiatry, 20,* 79–86.

Morris, C. (1946). *Signs, language and behavior.* New York: Prentice-Hall.

Morris, C. (1971). *Writings on the general theory of signs.* The Hague: Mouton.

Newman, S. S., & Mather, V. G. (1938). Analysis of spoken language of patients with affective disorders. *American Journal of Psychiatry, 94,* 913–942.

Newman, S. S. (1939). Personal symbolism in language patterns. *Psychiatry, 2,* 177–182.

Ng, S. H., & Bradac, J. J. (1993). *Power in language.* Newbury Park, CA: Sage.

Ogden, C. K., & Richards, I. A. (1947). *The meaning of meaning* (rev. ed.). New York: Harcourt, Brace & World.

Osgood, C. E. (1956). *Method and theory in experimental psychology.* New York: Oxford University Press.

Osgood, C. E., & Sebeok, T.A. (1954). *Psycholinguistics.* Supplement to *The Journal of Abnormal and Social Psychology* (also, Indiana University Publications in Anthropology and Linguistics, Memoir 10)

Osgood, C. E., Suci, G., & Tannenbaum, P. (1957). *The measurement of meaning.* Urbana: University of Illinois Press.

OSS Assessment Staff. (1948). *Assessment of men: Selection of personnel for the office of strategic services.* New York: Holt, Rinehart, & Winston.

Piaget, J. (1920/1926). *The language and thought of the child.* New York: Harcourt, Brace & World.

Pittenger, R. E. (1958). Linguistic analysis of tone of voice in communication of affect. *Psychiatric Research Reports 8,* 41–53.

Pittenger, R. E., Hockett, C. F., & Danehy, J. J. (1960). *The first five minutes.* Ithaca, NY: Martineau.

Pittenger, R. E. & Smith, H. L., Jr. (1957). A basis for some contributions of linguistics to psychiatry. *Psychiatry, 20,* 61–78.

Potter, J., & Wetherell, M. (1987). *Discourse and social psychology: Beyond attitudes and behaviour.* London: Sage.

Rosenthal, R. (1966). *Experimenter effects in behavioral research.* New York: Appleton-Century-Crofts.

Rosenthal, R. (Ed.). (1979). *Skill in nonverbal communication: Individual differences.* Cambridge, MA: Oelgeshlager, Gunn, and Hain.

Rosenthal, R. (1985). Nonverbal cues in the mediation of interpersonal expectancy effects. In A.W. Siegman & S. Feldstein (Eds.), *Multichannel integrations of nonverbal behavior* (pp. 105–28) Hillsdale, NJ: Lawrence Erlbaum Associates.

Rosenthal, R., Hall, J. A., DiMatteo, M. R, Rogers, P. L., & Archer, D. (1979). *Sensitivity to nonverbal communication: The PONS test.* Baltimore: Johns Hopkins University Press.

Ryan, E. B., & Giles, H. (1982). *Attitudes to language variation: Social and applied contexts.* London: Edward Arnold.

Sanford, F. H. (1941). *Individual differences in the mode of verbal expression.* Unpublished manuscript. Harvard College Library.

Sanford, F. H. (1942a). Speech and personality. *Psychological Bulletin, 30,* 811–845.

Sanford, F. H. (1942b). Speech and personality: A comparative case study. *Character and Personality, 10,* 169–198.

Sapir, E. (1921). *Language.* New York: Harcourt Brace.

Sapir, E. (1927). Speech as a personality trait. *American Journal of Sociology, 32,* 892–905. Reprinted in D. G. Mandlebaum (1949). *Selected writings of Edward Sapir.* Berkeley: University of California Press.

Saussure, F. de (1974). *Course in general linguistics.* London: Fontana.

Scheflen, A. E. (1965). Quasi-courtship behavior in psychotherapy. *Psychiatry, 28,* 245–257.

Scherer, K. R. (1978). Personality inference from voice quality: The loud voice of extroversion. *European Journal of Social Psychology, 8,* 467–487.

Scherer, K. R. (1979). Personality markers in speech. In K. R. Scherer & H. Giles (Eds.), *Social markers in speech* (pp. 147–209). Cambridge: Cambridge University Press.

Scherer, K. R. (Ed.). (1988). *Facets of emotion: Recent research.* Hillsdale, NJ: Lawrence Erlbaum.

Scherer, K. R., & Giles, H. (Eds.). (1979). *Social markers in speech.* Cambridge: Cambridge University Press.

Schutz, W. C. (1966). *The interpersonal underworld.* Palo Alto, CA: Science & Behavior Books.

Searle, J. R. (1969). *Speech acts: An essay in the philosophy of language.* Cambridge: Cambridge University Press.

Searle, J. R. (1979). *Expression and meaning: Studies in the theory of speech acts.* Cambridge: Cambridge University Press.

Sebeok, T. A. (1977). Zoosemiotic components of Human Communication. In T. A. Sebeok (Ed.), *How animals communicate.* Bloomington: Indiana University Press. Reprinted in R. E. Innis, (Ed.), (1985), *Semiotics: An Introductory Anthology. Bloomington:* Indiana University Press (pp. 294–324).

Sebeok, T. A. (1990). Indexicality. *The American Journal of Semiotics,* 7(4), 7–28.

Segall, M. H., Campbell, D. T. & Herskovits, M. J. (1966). *The influence of culture on visual perception.* New York: Bobbs-Merrill.

Semin, G. R., & Fiedler, K. (1988). The cognitive functions of linguistic categories in describing persons: Social cognition and language. *Journal of Personality and Social Psychology, 54,* 558–567.

Siegman, A. W., & Feldstein, S. (1987). *Nonverbal behavior and communication.* New York: Lawrence Erlbaum.

Siegman, A.W. (1978/1987). The telltale voice: Nonverbal messages of verbal communication. In A. W. Siegman & S. Feldstein (Eds.), *Nonverbal behavior and communication* (pp. 351–434). New York: Lawrence Erlbaum.

Skinner, B. F. (1957). *Verbal behavior.* New York: Appleton-Century-Crofts.

Soskin, W. F., & John, V. P. (1963). The study of spontaneous talk. In R. G. Barker (Ed.), *The stream of behavior.* New York: Appleton-Century-Crofts.

Southard, E. E. (1916). On descriptive analysis of manifest delusions from the subject's point of view. *Journal of Abnormal Psychology, 2,* 189–202.

Stern, W. (1925). *Zeitschrift für pädagogishe Psychologie,* 25, 110–112.

Tajfel, H., & Turner, J. C. (1979). An integrative theory of intergroup conflict. In W.G. Austin & S. Worchel (Eds.), *The social psychology of intergroup relations.* Monterey, CA: Brooks/Cole.

Trager, G. L. (1958). Paralanguage: A first approximation. *Studies in Linguistics, 13,* 1–12.

Triandis, H. C. (1994). *Culture and social behavior.* New York: McGraw-Hill.

Turner, J. C. (Ed.). (1987). *Rediscovering the social group: A self-categorization theory*. Oxford: Blackwell.
Weber, R. P. (1990). *Basic content analysis*. Newbury Park, CA: Sage Publications.
White, L. (1959). The concept of culture. *American Anthropologist*, 61, 227–251.
Winer, B. J. (1962). *Statistical principles in experimental design*. New York: McGraw-Hill.

Index

BERKELEY INSIGHTS IN LINGUISTICS AND SEMIOTICS

Irmengard Rauch
General Editor

Through the publication of ground-breaking scholarly research, this series deals with language and the multiple and varied paradigms through which it is studied. Language as viewed by linguists represents micrometa-approaches that intersect with macrometa-approaches of semiotists who understand language as an inlay to all experience. This data-based series bridges study of the sciences with that of the humanities. Monographs of at least 200 pages are invited by the General Editor, University of California—Berkeley, Department of German, Berkeley, California 94720.